Praise for *ADHD*

'This book is a must-read for every parent or teacher of a child with ADHD. This fantastic guide will leave you feeling more confident with everyday situations and the battles we face raising neurodivergent children'
Lisa Lloyd, author of *Raising the SEN-Betweeners*

'Jessie emerges as a guiding voice for parents of neurodivergent children. Her deep empathy and commitment to nurturing every child's potential shine throughout the book. This is the book I wish my parents had'   **Kate Lister, historian and journalist**

'This essential guide offers clear, practical advice to help parents understand ADHD, support their child's unique strengths with joy and confidence and feel less alone while navigating the often daunting diagnosis process – without blame or judgement'
Zenna Hopson, former chairman of Ofsted

'Jessie Hewitson is the calm and trusted voice parents of neurodivergent children need. This book, with its focus on understanding and practical tips, is a great investment in your child's well-being for anyone parenting an ADHD child'
Ed Archer, Chairman of the PDA Society

'A must-read for parents of kids with ADHD. Jessie writes in such a sensitive and easy-to-digest way. This book will give you a much greater understanding of ADHD and your child'
George Lewis, comedian, actor, writer and presenter

'Parents and teachers are longing for a straightforward, easy-to-read, expert book on ADHD – a go-to place where everything you need to know is right there. This book is it'
Carrie Grant MBE, broadcaster, author and coach

'*ADHD* takes us on a courageous journey through the challenges in the long process of raising any neurodivergent child, but specifically one with ADHD. Hewitson asks and authoritatively answers all of the questions we ourselves would want to ask. This is a very human and very needed guide to this lifelong ADHD journey for both parent and child'

Dr William Dodson, LF-APA, psychiatrist

'An incredibly practical and detailed exploration of ADHD, childhood and parenthood – vital for all adults who spend any time with children. A must-read' **Pete Wharmby,**
author of *Untypical* and *What I Want to Talk About*

'As a parent, journalist, campaigner and author, Jessie has been a tireless champion of neurodivergent young people. This book will be essential reading for those seeking to better understand and support children who think differently'

Jolanta Lasota, Chief Executive of Ambitious about Autism

'An amazingly researched and accessible manual on how to navigate life with an ADHD child'

Camilla Pang, scientist and author of *Explaining Humans*

Jessie Hewitson is an author, award-winning journalist and co-founder of NeuroUniverse, a company that provides training for companies in neurodiversity. She lives in north London with her (very) Welsh husband, her two children and her cat, who urgently needs an autism assessment.

Also by Jessie Hewitson

Autism: How to Raise a Happy Autistic Child

ADHD

How to Raise a Happy ADHD Child

JESSIE HEWITSON

First published in Great Britain in 2025 by Orion Spring,
an imprint of The Orion Publishing Group Ltd
Carmelite House, 50 Victoria Embankment
London EC4Y 0DZ
An Hachette UK Company

The authorised representative in the EEA is Hachette Ireland,
8 Castlecourt Centre, Dublin 15, D15 XTP3 Ireland (email: info@hbgi.ie)

SRD

A CIP catalogue record for this book is available from the British Library.

ISBN (Trade Paperback) 978 1 3987 2453 2
ISBN (Ebook) 978 1 3987 2454 9
ISBN (Audio) 978 1 3987 2455 6

Printed and bound in India by Manipal Technologies Limited, Manipal

MIX
Paper | Supporting
responsible forestry
FSC™ C104740

www.orionbooks.co.uk

*This book is dedicated to the amazing M,
owner of one of the two best ADHD brains in the world.
Love wave!*

Contents

Introduction

My son, M, was eight when his ADHD was diagnosed. The news came as no surprise, least of all to him. He had identified it himself at the age of five after a school assembly on neurodiversity. 'Mum, I have DHD,' he told me firmly, rushing in from school that day, having rung the doorbell five times in a row and thrown his rucksack on the hallway floor (and not on the hook I ask him to hang it up on every morning).

'They told us about it in school and EVERYTHING they said about it was ME!' he shouted, before legging it into the lounge to play Xbox with his brother, still in his wet raincoat – who knew when and where that would come off?

My husband and I had a little chuckle about M's announcement: how his focus in the assembly had wandered somewhere else when it came to the A part of ADHD. Then we stopped. Because what if he was right? What if our quirky, hilarious, one-off child had attention deficit hyperactivity disorder?

The years that followed were punctuated by regular calls home from school to have chats about M's behaviour, and his teacher opened one parents' evening meeting with a sigh: 'Where on earth to start?'

And so he went on the NHS waiting list to have an assessment. I began to tell friends in the pub casually that we were anticipating a diagnosis but we weren't worried. I had written a book on neurodiversity, after all, and prided myself on my progressive views in this area. Then, three years after the famous school assembly, the email landed in my inbox from the psychiatrist with the result of M's assessment.

I clicked on it and went to battle with Egress, the madly complicated secure messaging software the medical profession insists on using, to open the document. And there it was, confirmed in black and white. My wonderful son – the funniest child ever to walk the streets of north London – officially had ADHD.

I had expected to feel . . . not much. Perhaps relief that I could give M the news. He had been frustrated to have to wait so long for some doctor to tell him what he already knew.

But instead, I felt fear and anxiety. One half of my brain was telling me the news was nothing but valuable signposting to help him navigate life among the neurotypicals (people who don't have ADHD or autism). But the other part was working overtime. Suddenly, my high-minded perspective on the issue had fractured, vanished.

Would he be able to knuckle down and keep a job, do the boring tasks that are required in building a career? Would he ever find listening easy? Had I not been recognising his anxiety, mistaking it instead for confidence or boisterousness? Would he end up on medication that is, basically, amphetamines – speed, which I (kids, Mum, look away) took at university and which once kept me awake for two days straight?

The worry stayed with me for days. Then, as the fog cleared, I managed to pinpoint what it was that had startled me so unexpectedly. I was worrying that it meant M wouldn't be happy. Which would mean, by extension, that I couldn't be either.

Somewhere along the way, my brain had subconsciously linked ADHD with unhappiness. I hadn't been aware of it when the idea of my son having the condition was theoretical. But as soon as it turned out to be what was *actually happening*, what was submerged rose to the surface.

Introduction

Over the next 250 pages, I'm going to suggest that the way to parent an ADHD child is to focus on helping them be happy.

Of course, no one has the magic recipe for bringing up a happy child, but after ten years of research, I've come up with the basic ingredients. The late psychotherapist Jasmine El-Doori, in a conversation we had shortly before she died, defined love as making an effort to understand another person.

As parents, we can assume that we understand our children as we spend so much time with them, but sometimes that isn't enough. Particularly if your child has a hidden disability, such as ADHD, and especially if you have a different brain type. Understanding a child thrown into a complicated situation – born into a world that hasn't been built for them and doesn't understand how their brain works differently – can require work, an open mind and research. This book is intended to act as a shortcut, as I've done a lot of the work and research for you.

Other ingredients are to get the support at school right and to help your child lose any shame, which is an all-too-common emotion felt by some adult ADHDers after a lifetime of being told they are lazy, naughty, too much. Help them build a strong core belief within them that having ADHD is part of who they are and that it makes them no worse and no better than someone who does not have ADHD.

As for me, I've had to learn how to communicate differently with my son; how to parent differently. Because of M's big personality, I had seen only self-confidence, when really all the noise and activity had masked a lot of anxiety, confusion and dysregulation. It was a painful process and involved quite intense feelings of guilt for not having worked these things out sooner. The coat, shoes and bags still never get to where they need to be – not without my help – but hey, the world is an imperfect place.

When we finally told M the news of his diagnosis, he smiled. His older brother, E, who you might remember from my last book, *Autism: How to Raise a Happy Autistic Child*, wandered over, gave him a hug and said: 'Let your wonderful ADHD brain shine.'

Some Terms Explained

Neurotypical: someone who isn't an ADHDer or autistic or isn't neurodivergent

Neurodiverse: this is the fact of a diversity of brain types, it is not a term that describes people

Neurodivergent: a person who has a brain type that is different from that of a neurotypical. An autistic person or ADHDer is neurodivergent

Autistic: I refer to autistic people only as autistic, not as 'having autism', for the same reason that gay people don't 'have homosexuality', they are gay. It's part of who they are, not a condition to be treated

ADHD: I have sometimes had to say 'people with ADHD' despite the above, as the alternative, 'being an ADHDer', is too grammatically clunky for this writer to bear

AuDHD: the term for when someone has a double whammy of neurodivergence, as they are both autistic and an ADHDer

No disorders here: where possible I have tried not to refer to any neurodivergent conditions as disorders, but I've been limited with ADHD as there isn't an alternative name for it . . . yet.

1

Defining ADHD

What is ADHD? A good start surely is the definition of the condition in the diagnostic bible that is the American Psychiatric Association's *Diagnostic and Statistical Manual of Mental Disorders*, 5th edition (*DSM-5*). This is the book used by clinicians to diagnose our children based on its criteria, and it defines ADHD like this:

> [Attention deficit hyperactivity disorder] is a neurodevelopmental disorder defined by impairing levels of inattention, disorganization, and/or hyperactivity-impulsivity. Inattention and disorganization entail inability to stay on task, seeming not to listen, and losing materials necessary for tasks, at levels that are inconsistent with age or developmental level. Hyperactivity-impulsivity entails overactivity, fidgeting, inability to stay seated, intruding into other people's activities, and inability to wait – symptoms that are excessive for age or developmental level.

However, while researching this book, it's become increasingly obvious to me how flawed this definition is. 'Impairing levels of attention', for example – is this always true? It isn't, because the answer will differ depending on the context. Observe my son in an English lesson and you'll see a child with a short attention span. But watch him at home playing *Minecraft* (or, when he was younger, drawing), and his capacity for attention is likely to be far higher than any of his neurotypical peers.

That the condition is summarised in its name as 'attention deficit' is misleading and in part to blame for me not getting my son assessed sooner. He was five and I thought, 'He can't have ADHD when he draws intently for half an hour while sitting down, can he?' (Answer: he very definitely can, as we realised years later after things got very tough at school.)

And then there is the 'H' part of ADHD, which is just as prob-lematic as the 'AD'. What 'hyperactivity' misses is the fact that lots of people who are diagnosed with ADHD won't be. Hyper-active, I mean. The National Institute for Health and Care Excellence (NICE) reports that between 20 and 30 per cent of people with ADHD – often female – are diagnosed with the 'in-attentive' and not the 'hyperactive' presentation of ADHD. And once young people get past the age of fourteen – whatever their gender – they don't show much overt hyperactivity, according to Dr William Dodson, a US-based psychiatrist who is one of the most respected names in the ADHD world.

Also, for reasons we'll get on to, ADHD is not (in my mind) a disorder: it's a brain difference. So what we're left with is that not one single letter in ADHD is correct. And this is partly because the *DSM-5*'s summary of the condition peers into it from the out-side. You could argue that this must be the case – it's a manual that psychiatrists and other professionals use to make a diagno-sis based on how the patient before them is presenting. But the result is that the definition is very surface-level. The most likely reason why it's not yet informed by the inside stuff too is that most of the research has historically been led by people without ADHD, who don't fully understand the lived experience, and for anything to be included in the *DSM-5* it needs a body of research.

The end result is that the focus on physical hyperactivity is front and centre of the *DSM*'s definition because it's the bit that everyone can clearly see (in the 70–80 per cent who have it, assuming they are under the age of fourteen), and it's the bit that sometimes annoys neurotypicals. But there's barely any mention of the mental hyperactivity that accompanies ADHD 100 per cent of the time, whatever type of ADHD you are identified with. And the *DSM-5*'s very narrow and inaccurate view sets the tone for how the world sees ADHD: diagnosticians use it, and schools, work and society in general absorbs its messages.

Let's take a look at the second part of the *DSM-5* definition: 'Hyperactivity-impulsivity entails overactivity, fidgeting, inability to stay seated, intruding into other people's activities, and inability to wait.' It's possible to rewrite the above in a more objective, accurate way, as I've done below. It expresses the same points but is better at conveying both how ADHD looks *and* feels.

Mental hyperactivity is always present, sometimes combined with physical hyperactivity. Both states are accompanied by a feeling of restlessness. Being expected to stay still for long periods can be stressful and taxing, as can trying not to interrupt, in a bid to articulate thoughts quickly before they vanish.

Crucially, this definition is also free of value judgements – and this is the last major problem with how the *DSM-5* sees ADHD. The *DSM-5* is not a neutral assessment of ADHD; it's measuring ADHD brains against neurotypical ones, and anything that strays too far from neurotypical is labelled disordered. It talks about ADHD young people 'intruding' on the activities of others – ADHDers are portrayed as irritants, disturbing other people's work and peace.

3

Andy Smith, someone who you will hear from throughout this book, is the founder of Spectrum Gaming, a support group for young neurodivergent people. An autistic man who is on a long waiting list to be assessed for ADHD, he is working with local authorities and developing research into why autistic and ADHD young people often find school so difficult; he is becoming a leading voice for a younger generation of neurodivergents. He points out that when it comes to 'minority brain types', things tend to be seen only in the negative, when there are positives too. Smith references a talk given by Edward Hallowell – a well-known American psychiatrist and ADHDer, now in his seventies – hosted by the ADHD Foundation in 2021. 'Hallowell pointed out that ADHDers are labelled as distractible, but that also means being curious, because you can spot things other people have missed and discover new things other people have not noticed,' he says. 'Impulsive? When you think about it, creativity is impulsivity gone right – every time someone has created or invented something, that comes from someone being impulsive. In the right setting, it can be a great skill.'

Hallowell has also described ADHD as what happens when someone has the brain of a Ferrari but the brakes of a bicycle. Smith adds: 'With the Ferrari brain, if it's something you're focused on, you can do an amazing job, but your bicycle brakes can put you in difficult situations, when you can be quite impulsive and struggle with attention.'

Smith believes there are challenges and advantages whether you are ADHD or not. The upsides of being neurotypical include being able to read between the lines and the ability to be socially strategic, he says. The downsides are that you are illogical and obsessed by conformity. He points to a quote he loves from the X account Autistic Not Weird: 'So why do people say you're the weird one? Because there's more of them than you.'

One thing absent from the *DSM-5* definition of ADHD is any mention of hyperfocus – perhaps because it isn't consistent with the manual's view of a condition defined by its lack of attention. While it is true that ADHD can come with a high degree of distractibility, it can also bring next-level focus skills. Hyperfocus is an unsung positive and, it seems increasingly obvious, a central feature for neurodivergent people of all stripes.

It's high time ADHD had a rebrand. The *DSM* will have to change its definition at some point, I'm certain of it – and as a result the name given to ADHD. Given the inaccuracy of the hyperactivity aspect, not to mention the way the manual looks at so-called attention deficiency and the fact that treating it as a disorder is increasingly unsustainable, they're going to need a whole new acronym, in fact.

And yet I don't think there will ever be a name that everyone will get on board with, not when it's intended to encapsulate so many people (400 million adults alone as of 2020). But the definition and name can – and should – be improved. Below is one alternative definition being used by some neurodivergent people.

MONOTROPISM

Monotropism is a theory put forward by three neurodivergent scholars – Dinah Murray, Wenn Lawson and Mike Lesser – to describe the laser focus that some people can pay to a small number of things at one time, to the exclusion of everything else. This theory has been embraced by the autistic community as a central explanation of their lives, and more recently is being explored as a central theme for ADHDers also.

Polytropic people – which is likely to mean neurotypical – can spread their attention thinly. They may find it easier to chat to someone about whether they want tea, then return to the work they were doing (relatively easily) for five minutes before they have a meeting. This is not what it's like for a monotropic person, who will have spent ages trying to focus, only to have someone force their attention elsewhere with the tea chat. The switching of attention may have been a stressful process, followed by difficulty reconnecting with the task, which may take some time. Generally monotropics just want to crawl into their attention tunnel and stay there hidden until they are ready to come out.

And if you believe that monotropism is at the core of the autistic and ADHD experience, then it's easy to see why school – where pupils are cycled through different classrooms to sit (calmly, quietly and without fidgeting, please!) in front of different teachers who teach them different subjects – is so difficult.

I interviewed Dinah Murray, the autistic woman behind the theory of monotropism, for my last book, *Autism*. She explained how stressful back-and-forth conversations can be for a monotrope: demands are being placed on you to move your attention to places you don't want it to go. She added that when teaching a monotropic child, it makes absolutely no sense *not* to start with their interests.

Some people now refer to themselves as being monotropic rather than having ADHD or being autistic, as a rejection of the labels applied to them by the medical establishment. 'The way I see ADHD is through the lens of monotropism,' says Andy Smith. 'Most people can focus their attention on lots of things a little bit, but ADHDers focus on one thing a lot. Some people say they can switch off and I'm like: "How do you do that?" I need a distraction to get myself to sleep otherwise my thoughts are too much.'

THE ROLE OF ENVIRONMENT AND THE SOCIAL MODEL OF DISABILITY

Environment plays an enormous part in how well ADHDers cope (or don't). This explains why someone with ADHD can find life very difficult in some contexts, whereas in others they can thrive. The social model of disability explains why focusing on environment is the best way to support a child. For example: instead of sending them to a school where massive adult support and interventions are necessary to cope, do they just need to be in a school that doesn't stress them out as much?

Where the pathology paradigm asks, 'What is wrong with the individual?', the social model of disability asks, 'What's wrong with the person's environment?', writes Jill Enright, in a piece for the website Medium. 'When a person encounters difficulties, the social model does not ask what is wrong with the person. Instead, this model points to the context and surrounding environment. The social model seeks to uncover and change how institutions and cultural norms disable individuals due to a lack of understanding, acceptance, and accommodation.'

What is neurodiversity?

The term 'neurodiversity' was coined by journalist Harvey Blume in 1997, after discussions with other autistic people in online groups, and then popularised by the Australian sociologist Judy Singer in her undergraduate thesis at the University of Technology in Sydney. While the *Oxford English Dictionary* defines a disorder as an illness or condition that 'disrupts normal physical or mental functions', Blume and Singer argued that it is more helpful to think of difference as a natural occurrence rather than a symptom of a brain gone wrong. They argue that diversity of the human mind is a biological fact.

Nick Walker, the autistic academic, has written the following definition on her website:

1 Neurodiversity is a natural and valuable form of human diversity.

2 The idea that there is one 'normal' or 'healthy' type of brain or mind, or one 'right' style of neurocognitive functioning, is a culturally constructed fiction, no more valid (and no more conducive to a healthy society or to the overall well-being of humanity) than the idea that there is one 'normal' or 'right' ethnicity, gender or culture.

3 The social dynamics that manifest in regard to neurodiversity are similar to the social dynamics that manifest in regard to other forms of human diversity (e.g., diversity of ethnicity, gender or culture). These dynamics include the dynamics of social power inequalities, and also the dynamics by which diversity, when embraced, acts as a source of creative potential.

In an interview, Walker added that the concept of a 'normal mind' is as absurd and innately oppressive as the idea that white people are the default 'normal' race or that hetero-sexuality is the one 'normal' sexuality.

Amen to that. Let's challenge the aspiration for our kids to be normal. It can encourage us to experience something like a sense of loss when our kids are identified as not normal, but there is also dislocation, a feeling of unreality. This is what my child ought to be like, this is what I was expecting them to be, this is what other children are, this is what my child is not. Normal is life for the great mass of parents who aren't going through what you and your family are going through.

Of course I understand why parents wish their ADHD children were normal (I certainly did when my eldest was diagnosed as autistic when he was two). On the most basic level, it's a lot easier for them – in terms of fitting in at school, learning and friendships – and ditto for parents, as your child isn't being constantly buffeted by the world. But although it might be easy in the short term (until you've accepted your difference), it also comes with downsides: it's boring, for a start, and restrictive. Certain people insist on it, look askance at those who step outside the narrow boundaries of their experiences, and it gives them a fixed and judgemental outlook on life.

Jonathan Mooney wrote a book entitled *Normal Sucks*. Diagnosed with ADHD and dyslexia, he didn't learn to read until he was twelve. School was a struggle until he realised that he wasn't the problem – the system and the concept of normal were. His book looks at the toll that being 'not normal' takes on kids and adults when they're trapped in environments that label them, shame them and tell them, even in subtle ways, that they are the problem.

Let's teach our kids instead to see that being normal is the very least they can be – middle-of-the-road, literally mediocre. Ask them to name one person who has changed the world by being extremely normal. One of the worst insults my wonderful cousins in New Zealand taught me was: 'God, you're average!'

2

A History of ADHD in
Ten People

When my son M was diagnosed with ADHD, I thought I knew what that meant. Having written a book on autism, I reckoned I had a pretty good handle on neurodivergence. Except I didn't, and it was only when M stopped being able to go to school that I was forced to face up to this painful fact.

Researching this chapter provided some consolation for people like me, perhaps like you, who think they know all about ADHD. Because it's clear I'm far from alone in my ignorance. The history of ADHD is littered with doctors only scraping the surface of what it means to have this brain type. Non-ADHD doctors have wasted three centuries stroking their beards and discussing the condition among themselves – going round in circles, observing what is clearly visible and failing to consider what might be invisible – because naturally it would be madness to ask ADHD people about it, listen to what they say and take it seriously.

What I really wanted to learn in writing this book was the reasons this neurotype is so stigmatised, perhaps the most stigmatised condition of all. And writing this chapter, it hit me: it's because it's so poorly understood. As the official description of ADHD doesn't precisely nail what ADHD is, it doesn't always ring true with the general public. It's been too easy to argue that it's all wrong.

I found it helpful to know that the controversy we are mired in today – with many people believing ADHD is overdiagnosed, others doubting it is even real – has already happened Stateside. In the US in the 1980s, mums and dads like us read the same kind of newspaper and magazine articles we find ourselves nervously scanning today: about neurotic parents who slap labels on their kids, pathologise them, find medical explanations for natural behaviours.

Perhaps those parents, the ones doing the reading, doubted their own feelings too, this awareness that their child was different. Perhaps they too beat themselves up after their son or daughter hit crisis point, wondering why things had to get to this stage before they were able to acknowledge or uncover the extent to which their child had been struggling. This is how I feel. How did I not notice the invisible bits of ADHD: the constant feeling of restlessness in my son, that his brain was in overdrive, leaving him the opposite of hyperactive – frequently knackered, in fact – and his corrosive feelings of shame? It feels like these bits aren't discussed nearly as much as they should be.

I'm hoping this potted history will give you confidence in your judgement. For starters, it will show you that there have always been people with ADHD. This is a counter-argument to the people who claim it is caused by social media, processed food or too much screen time, as it existed way before any of these things were invented. We have to ignore the armchair experts in the same way as parents in the US in the 1980s had to ignore the angry Scientologists (my favourite type of Scientologist . . . more on this later).

But one person who shouldn't have been ignored was the first to talk about what would later be known as ADHD, Alexander Crichton. Crichton had the valuable insight that any difficulties ADHD kids were having at school were not necessarily their fault but that of the education they were receiving. That particular nugget has only been around since the 1790s. Any day now, let's hope someone will take notice . . .

In the following pages, we will meet ten people who changed the way I think about ADHD, and I hope they will for you too.

SIR ALEXANDER CRICHTON
AND 'THE FIDGETS'

A Scottish physician working in the eighteenth and nineteenth centuries, Sir Alexander Crichton became the personal doctor of Tsar Alexander I of Russia. He is thought to be the first person to describe children with difficulties around distractibility, lack of sustained attention and poor inhibition. Unlike his colleagues, Crichton did not form any judgement over whether these children's behaviour was moral or not. He saw their differences as physiological in nature, rather than being born out of sin.

In his book *An Inquiry into the Nature and Origin of Mental Derangement*, published in 1798 and written while working in hospitals in Paris, Stuttgart and Vienna, Crichton noted a 'mental restlessness' among some of his patients, and concluded that the malaise was either congenital or the result of brain damage caused by disease, which diminished in adulthood. He noted: 'The barking of dogs, an ill-tuned organ or the scolding of women are sufficient to distract patients of this description to such a degree as almost approaches to the nature of delirium. When people are affected in this manner, which they very frequently are, they have a particular name for the state of their nerves . . . They say they have the fidgets.'

He also studied the impact of education. But rather than focus on the child and their so-called deficiencies, he looked at their environment and what it was about it that made focusing so hard. So instead of 'fixing' the learner, Crichton proposed improving education.

13

SIR GEORGE FREDERIC STILL
AND AN 'EXAGGERATION OF EXCITABILITY'

In March 1902, Sir George Frederic Still, dubbed 'the father of modern paediatrics', presented a series of lectures to the Royal Society of Medicine in London in which he described 'an abnormal defect of moral control in children'. These lectures are considered by many to be the starting point in the formal history of a condition that would later become known as ADHD.

In his lectures, he discussed observations of fifteen cases – ten boys and five girls – who displayed the following symptoms: '(1) passionateness [impulsivity]; (2) spitefulness – cruelty; (3) jealousy; (4) lawlessness; (5) dishonesty; (6) wanton mischievousness – destructiveness; (7) shamelessness – immodesty; (8) sexual immorality; and (9) viciousness'. He added: 'The keynote of these qualities is self-gratification, the immediate gratification of self without regard either to the good of others or to the larger and more remote good of self.'

Still very clearly viewed the condition through the lens of morality. Describing the children he observed as having 'defective' moral control – and arguing that moral control was necessary for the public good – the implication was that these kids were selfish, bordering on malevolent.

However, where he did agree with Crichton was that ADHD traits were biological in nature, so on the upside, it allowed for people to begin to realise that punishing children for these behaviours wouldn't 'fix' them. Still's work was influential, and medical professionals busied themselves to find the biological mechanisms of the condition. The race was on to find out what caused what would later be known as ADHD.

FRANZ KRAMER AND HANS POLLNOW

In 1932, the German physicians Franz Kramer and Hans Poll-now wrote a paper entitled 'A hyperkinetic disease of infancy' ('Eine hyperkinetische Erkrankung im Kindesalter'). The primary characteristic of this disease was a 'marked motor restlessness', with activities appearing very urgent.

This aimlessness and desire for quickly changing activities was due to distractibility by new and intensive stimuli, the doctors decided.

But while the children showed no perseverance in their activities – playing no game for more than a few minutes – the physicians also noticed their young patients could spend hours on activities that interested them, a nuance that appears to have fallen down the back of the medical sofa over the years.

However, for parents burdened with any lingering doubt that the condition was a universally Bad Thing for their offspring, Kramer and Pollnow said that hyperkinetic children were often disobedient, had severe educational problems, struggled to play harmoniously with other children and were generally unpopular among their peers. The work of Kramer and Pollnow was highly influential and ensured that the main focus of this condition was squarely on the traits of hyperactivity, a focus that remains today.

CHARLES BRADLEY

In 1937, Charles Bradley, the medical director of what is now known as Bradley Hospital, in Rhode Island, US – founded by his great-uncle, George Bradley, to treat neurologically impaired children – reported a positive effect of stimulant medication in patients hospitalised for emotional and learning problems, who might today be diagnosed with ADHD.

It was a fluke. Bradley had invented a way of getting clearer brain scans, known as 'air encephalography', by drawing out cerebrospinal fluid – the fluid that flows in and around the hollow spaces of the brain and spinal cord – and replacing it with air. A side effect of this procedure was intense headaches, and for this he prescribed Benzedrine, believing that because Benzedrine is a stimulant, it would stimulate the fluid to replace itself. While it failed to help with the headaches, it did affect the behaviour and school performance of some of his patients. Having set up a systematic trial involving thirty of the hospital's younger patients, he observed remarkable improvements. They 'were more interested in their work and performed it more quickly and accurately', he reported. They were also less hyperactive, and some of them 'became emotionally subdued, without, however, losing interest in their surroundings'. There were benefits to their social lives too.

Bradley was surprised, to say the least, remarking: 'It appears paradoxical that a drug known to be a stimulant should produce subdued behavior in half of the children.' He later identified that children who were most likely to benefit from Benzedrine treatment were 'characterized by short attention span, dyscalculia [a learning disability related to numbers], mood lability, hyperactivity, impulsiveness and poor memory'.

MARGUERITE 'RITA' PANIZZON

Although Bradley and his colleagues published their pioneering discovery in prominent journals, their reports had almost no influence on research and practice for at least twenty-five years, possibly because they could not explain why stimulant medicines helped calm down fidgety children. Over time, however, the effect of stimulants began to be explored.

The most commonly used ADHD stimulant today, methylphenidate, was not initially promoted for hyperactive children when it first came to market in 1954 – instead it was sold as a tonic to treat mild depression and chronic fatigue, having been synthesised a decade earlier in Switzerland by the Italian chemist Leandro Panizzon. Back in the good old days, when taking new and potentially hazardous concoctions home for your family to sample was the done thing, Panizzon had asked his wife, Marguerite – known as Rita – to give the drug a shot before her tennis game. She came home full of praise. Its impact had been rapid: she had concentrated better and her game had improved. Panizzon was so delighted he named the drug after her: Ritalin.

NIKITA KHRUSHCHEV

On 4 October 1957, with the launch of the first man-made satellite into orbit around the Earth, the Space Race was won and it was clear who was the world's predominant scientific and technological power . . . and it wasn't the United States of America. While Nikita Khrushchev, the Soviet premier, celebrated the ascendancy of Sputnik 1 and the USSR, it sent a chill down US military spines, triggering a slew of questions about how America had been pipped to the post. It was clear to Washington that one thing was to blame: the liberal education system.

Or partly, at least. The trend in education in the States during the years leading up to the Cold War was child-led and focused on building life skills. Rather than being taught from a textbook, children might learn about botany by growing a vegetable garden. But the mighty US of A was not going to clobber the commies with weeny little courgettes and cress egg heads. No, sir. In order to beat the Soviets in the 'brain race', it was now decided there needed to be more focus on maths and science; students would have to stay in school for longer and achieve better grades. Nikita Khrushchev helped focus minds with his bolshie boasts about Soviet superiority.

So the progressive education approach was buried in a shallow grave among the baby carrots, and more traditional rote learning on core subjects – the type of thing ADHDers typically struggle with – took its place. Eleven months after the launch of Sputnik 1, and now with two more Russian satellites and one dog (poor Laika) orbiting the Earth, the $1 billion National Defense Education Act was passed. In order to create a generation of smarter kids that might help propel the US to dominance over the USSR, thousands of guidance counsellors were placed in schools to identify gifted children and to improve the chances of those who were struggling academically. Many of these underachievers exhibited the same characteristics: they were hyperactive, impulsive, inattentive, occasionally defiant. Sound familiar? Some pupils were directed to psychiatrists, who prescribed stimulant medication, and they were among the first to be unintentionally diagnosed with what we now call ADHD.

A year earlier, a new psychiatric condition had been identified, drawing on the work of Kramer and Pollnow: hyperkinetic impulse disorder. Although it made it into the *DSM-2*, the second edition of the American Psychiatric Association's *Diagnostic and Statistical Manual of Mental Disorders*, it merited just a single sentence: 'The disorder is characterized by overactivity, restlessness, distractibility and short attention span, especially in young children; the behavior usually diminishes by adolescence.'

Prior to this, children had to demonstrate extremely pronounced hyperactive, impulsive and often violent behaviour for a doctor to take notice. The new disorder drastically lowered this threshold, resulting in a definition that could be applied to pupils in most classrooms. Ritalin became licensed for use in children in 1962 and quickly became the preferred option for medication.

By the late 1960s, what we now call ADHD was the most common childhood psychiatric disorder in the US and Ritalin had become a bestseller for its manufacturer, Ciba, which engaged in a vigorous marketing campaign to promote its use.

VIRGINIA DOUGLAS

In a paper submitted to the Canadian Psychological Association detailing her experiences treating patients at the Montreal Children's Hospital, the late Canadian psychologist Virginia Douglas argued that deficits in sustained attention and impulse control were more significant features of the condition than hyperactivity.

Douglas's paper was influential, leading to a major rethink and, with the publication in 1980 of the DMS-3, a new diagnostic label: attention deficit disorder (ADD), with or without hyperactivity. An overabundance of energy and difficulty sitting still were no longer essential diagnostic criteria; now attention and impulse control got top billing. Hyperactivity fought its way back to star status in 1987, however, when the condition was renamed attention deficit hyperactivity disorder, with the three subtypes still used today: combined type, predominantly inattentive type and predominantly hyperactive-impulsive type.

MICHELE NOVOTNI

Adult ADHD did not exist until recently. 'It was thought of as a childhood disorder that one would outgrow,' recalls Michele Novotni, the psychologist and former president and CEO of the national Attention Deficit Disorder Association (ADDA), writing in *ADDitude* magazine. Novotni is based in the US and made it her mission to persuade people otherwise. 'Those of us who thought differently were professionally chastised,' she added.

In the 1990s, Novotni started writing books and articles proposing that adults could and did have ADHD. The American Psychological Association, the American Medical Association and the American Psychiatric Association all disagreed.

She explained in her article that in the days before the internet, she was part of a small group of people who travelled around the US, speaking at conferences and sharing information.

'One city at a time, we offered hope and help for adults who were struggling with something that didn't officially exist.' A member of the group, Stephen Copps, wrote one of the first books on treating adults who had ADD [the diagnosis before ADHD was coined] with medication. He was threatened with possible loss of his medical licence as he was a paediatrician and therefore not trained to work with adults. ADDA came to his defence and his licence was not revoked.

Astonishingly, discussion of adult ADHD was banned at some conferences until 2001. Novotni writes that she was the first person to be allowed to speak on the topic – but even then, the first time this happened she was relegated to a small room with an adjoining kitchen and bathroom because it was assumed there would be little interest. In the end, 'the room was flooded with people standing in the tub, sitting on the toilet, filling the halls and listening outside windows,' wrote Novotni. 'It was a pivotal event that marked the beginning of adult ADHD as a topic at conferences.'

L. RON HUBBARD

With straplines such as 'Ritalin helps the problem child become loveable again', the drug's ad campaign in the 1970s might best be described as questionable but effective: by the 1980s and 1990s, prescriptions had rocketed. Extensive soul-searching followed, with copious articles and hours of television devoted to looking at the reasons behind the rise in ADHD, with many perceiving it as a crisis of overdiagnosis.

Fears about Ritalin were amplified by the Church of Scientology, founded in 1952 by L. Ron Hubbard, which has a long history of opposition to psychiatry. Claims were made about the use and abuse of Ritalin, as well as a link to mental health crises and suicide. Many children were taken off their meds as a result.

In 2000, attorneys including John Coale – who has more recently worked with Donald Trump – participated in the cases, with Coale making the notorious claim: 'They were giving this stuff away like candy.'

Although all lawsuits were eventually dismissed, many people's reluctance to consider medication for their children can be traced to the discussions taking place around this time. And in many ways, the same questions are being asked today: are these ADHD diagnoses genuine? Are doctors pathologising kids who are just on the lively end of normal? Are drug companies cashing in on parental neuroses? Are mums and dads seeking a biological justification for their bratty children, when the answer lies in their own parenting?

3

Does My Child Have ADHD?

I spent years agonising over this question for my younger son. Very talkative: tick, he has ADHD. Can't sit down for dinner: tick. Fidgety: big tick. Draws quietly on his own for twenty minutes: cross, he doesn't have ADHD. Not always energetic, in fact can be very lethargic and impossible to gee up. For years I had an exhausting back-and-forth in my mind that would go nowhere. Is he? Isn't he?

Now I think: why did I place so much emphasis on what I thought? I'm not a bloody doctor. If my son was displaying signs of having a sore knee that wasn't going away, I wouldn't spend years wondering whether to get it looked at. I'd get on the phone to the GP, wait nineteen hours for someone to answer and ask the experts to decide.

Why is it different when we think our child may have ADHD? Partly, it is because the condition is relatable: some of its 'traits' are ones everyone shares, which makes it harder to distinguish if you are not a professional. All of us find it hard to focus at times, particularly on stuff that isn't naturally interesting to us. We have to make a conscious effort to smile and bite our lip when faced with someone who could bore for Britain and resist the urge to hurry them on so they get to the point a bit quicker. Most of us would say we can be disorganised.

But it's the extent of the issues and their impact on a person's life that differentiates those with ADHD from those without.

I wish my approach with my son all those years back had been to request the assessment first, then agonise over whether he was going to get a diagnosis. Say what you like about the long wait for an NHS consultation, at least it gives you plenty of time to think.

Because, to go back to the knee analogy, you shouldn't let your child get to the hobbling stage before doing something about it. And that's what I inadvertently did. I did the same with my elder son – had I asked for him to be assessed for ADHD when I first had thoughts about the condition, he might have been spared eight years or so of struggling to focus in class.

If ADHD came with less stigma attached – without the claims that it's being overdiagnosed or the sense that it's not a 'serious' condition – would we act more promptly? I think we would. Problems in the education system can play a part too. Your child's school might dismiss or play down your concerns because they don't know them as well as you do, or they simply don't see it, particularly if your child has a more inattentive presentation. But it could also be that seeing the issue will mean having to do something about it, and they either don't have the money, or the poor overworked SENCO (special educational needs coordinator) can't cope with adding another child to their caseload.

I wish M had been identified sooner than age eight – before the shame and anxiety of not being able to 'behave' in the expected way at school overwhelmed him. Ditto for E, star of my first book, who, because we were so blindly focused on his being autistic and who is more dreamy and inattentive, only got an ADHD diagnosis when he was thirteen.

This chapter heading may be 'Does My Child Have ADHD?' but remember: you don't need to decide. Only the doctor does.

WHAT ARE SOME OF THE SIGNS YOUR CHILD HAS ADHD?

Note: some of the below may not apply and your child may *still* have ADHD.

- They find it hard to stay still for long periods of time (unless doing something interesting).
- They are the owner of a racing brain that is easily distracted.
- They are a chatterbox and find it difficult to wait their turn to speak. There is a tendency to hijack the conversation.
- It is hard to wait before speaking: your child may feel like they will explode if they don't get to say their point, or forget what the point is if they don't get to say it quickly. (M would call out from bed when he was little: 'I have three things to say.' By the time we'd stumped across the landing, having left him for a bit to see if he'd go to sleep, some of the vital information he was ready to impart would have vanished from his mind, and he'd say when we arrived at his bedside: 'I've got two things to say . . .')
- They struggle to start, finish and generally organise tasks, giving up on them more quickly than neurotypical peers because it takes more effort.
- They find it difficult to listen and can get good at pretending to listen. (M is now more honest about this: 'I'm sorry, Mum, I didn't listen to a word you were saying.')
- There is a large amount of procrastination and leaving everything to the last minute – this is likely to make you, the parent, want to emit a primal scream every morning as you try to get your ADHD kid(s) ready for school.
- Your child needs lots of sensory input to settle – energy is noticeably calmer after a run around.

- Rather than sitting down as sofa-makers intended while watching a movie, they instead perch awkwardly on the back. My elder son, E, used to do this, resembling a cheetah flopping on a tree branch. It drove me nuts (I'm not sure now why it annoyed me so much). M was often upside-down, doing a kind of awkward handstand on the sofa while watching TV, often tumbling down.
- Inconsistent focus, not able to rely on their brain to pay attention, requiring lots of internal geeing-up ('Right, must concentrate'; 'Come on, brain!') when the task is boring.
- Speaking of which . . . yawn . . . often feeling bored. Especially at school. When I look back at videos of M when he was young, he's so often talking about how boring school is.
- Teachers say your child is bright but is not applying themselves.
- Extreme emotional reactions, which can provoke big emotional reactions in you, the parent. This certainly happens to me, and after I've shouted at a child and then felt ashamed of myself, I wonder, 'What would people who read my books think if they saw me now?' Just know that even people who write parenting books are doomed to fail at fairly regular intervals.
- A dreamy child frustrates you, the parent or carer, as you don't feel engaged with them. Talking to them is hard work – you feel you're not in the same room together. There is a lack of engagement with the outside world, as if the narrative inside their head is more compelling than what anyone else is doing.
- The ability to hyperfocus – focus intensely – on things of interest, often with brilliant outcomes.
- 'Out of the box' thinking and ability to find creative solutions. You may think there isn't a solution to a particular problem, only for your child to come up with one.
- Intelligence: a quick-acting brain making creative connections that are beyond the child's years. Donald Trump

has nothing on the negotiating prowess of M: the boy is a genius at spotting and using leverage.

- Higher energy levels, especially for tasks they are engaged with; zero energy for the ones they aren't.
- Difficulties maintaining friendships (making friends may be fine, but keeping them is another matter).
- Difficulty falling asleep. (And if this is you, speak to your doctor about whether your child can be prescribed the hormone melatonin, pronto.)
- Restless a lot of the time; feeling something that resembles anxiety much of the time, linked to the mental and physical hyperactivity; just not feeling calm.
- Extreme sensitivity to rejection or perceived rejection.
- Acting impulsively in friendships and relationships, which can lead to conflict.

Signs in older kids/teens might include:

- Risk-taking beyond what you would usually experience with teens. More likely to have unprotected sex, or drink, and this behaviour may be less due to acting out.
- Losing their belongings. A lot.
- Difficulty organising themselves for school: remembering which day to bring their science book, racing around the house just before school to find something. Bag never properly packed the night before – the very idea.
- Social difficulties, particularly for girls. Their peers may be exhibiting sophisticated friendship skills an ADHD child hasn't yet gained.
- Doing homework is a nightmare: it's difficult starting it, staying on track and not giving up. (Also remembering when it has to be done by – lots of remembering at 11 p.m. that they have to hand it in the next day.)

- The child may be viewed as immature by teachers and parents as they struggle to develop the same skills as their peers and refrain from impulsive behaviour.

THE THREE TYPES OF ADHD

The *DSM-5* separates ADHD into three subtypes (NB: not everyone believes that ADHD neatly divides itself this way, and possibly some people present differently at different times or different life stages or in different environments):

Predominantly inattentive: dreamy, zones out often; the inside of that person's brain is a much more attractive and comfortable place to be than the outside world.

Predominantly hyperactive-impulsive: frequently in motion, impatient, prone to interrupting; the kids that make their teachers sigh or worse.

Combined: both, or some parts of each.

Inattentive ADHD means you find it difficult to pay attention but don't outwardly seem hyperactive. An inattentive child struggles to expend effort and has brief and changing activities. They are a daydreamer, disorganised and forgetful, and there is likely to be a mismatch between their abilities and the grades they get. They may be consumed by their thoughts, which are so knotty they retreat from the world to untangle them. My elder son, now fourteen, used to have a very inattentive presentation (though this has changed as he's started taking medication). When little, he described the feeling of being totally absorbed in his thoughts, then re-emerging as though waking from a dream. I remember a stranger trying to give him instructions getting so frustrated that he clicked his fingers in his face and said, 'Wake up!' This inability to focus can lead to academic frustration, apathy, masking (i.e. pretending to be someone they're not – someone 'normal') and shame: 'Why can't I just knuckle down like everyone else?' It also annoys others (and the inattentive young person has to deal with the consequences of that; they most likely don't want to be dragged out of their thoughts and are wondering why people are giving them a hard time). This dream world is their natural habitat, such that hauling themselves out to rejoin the real world takes a huge amount of effort, especially when it is to do something boring, or if rejection or failure awaits.

Hyperactive and impulsive ADHD is easier to spot. These children are the ones who make their teacher's life difficult. They are impulsive and interrupt the class to voice the thought that simply will not wait quietly and patiently beneath a raised hand to be heard. They are the risk-takers and often the ones who get injured in the playground. I was always getting texts from the school informing me that M had bumped his head – this was so routine, I would get a shock on the days it didn't happen. One day I received a text within fifteen minutes of him being dropped off at school, which I thought was particularly impressive, given that he'd barely had time to take off his coat. These kids can struggle to make what teachers would call the 'correct' choices, and in less enlightened schools this leads to them being labelled naughty. Peers in the class may be frustrated by their disruptions. M and a friend thought it sensible very early on in their school career (while they were in a nursery attached to the local primary school) to get creative with the elements and add earth to the tadpole tank to see what would happen. An aquatic apocalypse is what. Uncomprehending, and just three years old, he was sent to see the headmistress for that. I'm sure the bereaved frogs would have approved. I certainly didn't.

Combined ADHD, as the name suggests, takes in both types. These children meet the criteria for both hyperactivity and inattentive ADHD.

HYPERACTIVE VS INATTENTIVE

'In clinic, we tend mostly to see the hyperactive-impulsive and combined categories, simply because they are more likely to cause problems for neurotypical people,' says Dr Helen Honey, a consultant psychiatrist at National Deaf Child and Adolescent Mental Health Services (CAMHS) in London who has ADHD herself. 'Whereas the inattentives don't cause problems for people other than themselves. Teachers don't see it. Only later on do you see low self-esteem and anxiety.'

Clinicians will often see the hyperactive-impulsive presentation in children and the inattentive presentation in adults. 'I do wonder if it morphs – perhaps the hyperactivity becomes less visible as people learn to mask more,' Dr Honey adds. 'As you get older, you get social cues saying, "Stop jumping on tables", or you get a job that is very active, so you have less need to be active outside of it.'

Inattentive ADHD is so poorly understood that unless you're really immersed in the ADHD world, it can look like laziness. 'It's difficult for people outside of this world to understand what is going on,' she says. 'We all have days when we're like that, so it's easy to think it's just the person being incompetent.'

Dr Honey also points out that people express their ADHD differently depending on their age and their sex. 'Girls may not be physically hyperactive but may be doodling, playing with their hair. With hyperactivity and impulsivity there can be real difficulty with relationships and keeping friendships. Typically, an ADHD child finds it easy to make friends but hard to maintain the friendship. Life can feel so boring that you provoke a situation so something can happen, or say something outrageous, or find it hard to keep secrets. You may also be an expert at pretending to listen, but you're trying so hard not to interrupt that you can't think of anything else but that. That level of energy can be difficult for other kids, as can someone getting into their personal space.'

WHAT ADHD LOOKS LIKE IN TEENS

Being a teenager is hard for anyone, but particularly for ADHDers. For kids who aren't mega hyperactive, the ADHD may not get picked up until they hit the moody years, when demands increase and the support reduces. This was true of my elder son, E. He was diagnosed as autistic at the age of two but wasn't identified as ADHD until he was thirteen. I'm kicking myself that it didn't happen sooner, though I recognise we were lucky to realise before the GCSE years. Really the ADHD was clearly there, I just didn't know enough about it to spot it.

Not only do you have exams, revision, coursework and home-work to contend with when you are a teenager, but the social demands become more complex, with peer relationships both more important and trickier to navigate. And in a mainstream school, the support will usually start to disappear, as the expect-ation is that the young person will be developing independence. 'Suddenly they need to manage their own timetable and home-work, and information is no longer given to parents, which reduces the opportunity for them to scaffold,' says Dr Honey. 'Socialising starts to become more fluid, with young people organising their own social lives, and it becomes less based around structured events. More hanging around in parks and each other's houses, which can be difficult if you have ADHD and/or are autistic.'

Compounding this are the brain changes in adolescents that make all young people on average more likely to take risks, more impulsive and more likely to shriek at you that you know nothing. 'Young people with ADHD are more likely to be at the extreme end of this, so may present with self-harming, drug use or other risky behaviour. ADHD looks quite different in teenagers than in younger children, and a lot of the problems are often put down to puberty or adolescence,' adds Dr Honey. 'It is important to keep an open mind about ADHD in young people who are struggling more than their peers.'

DON'T ALL YOUNG KIDS RESEMBLE ADHD KIDS?

While a lot of children are impulsive, hyperactive and inattentive – part and parcel of being young – the thing to look for is how they are compared with other children the same age.

'My kids were always in the accident book,' says Dr Honey. 'Perhaps parents can't take their child to the supermarket, or to church or on the bus, because they are noisy and can't sit down. Life begins to revolve around them and families find they have to start to make preparations based on past experience – yes, we can go to a restaurant as long as we bring the iPad so our child stays seated throughout the meal. The thing you'll notice is that your child requires extra adaptations to manage. Accidents, risky behaviours like running across roads, running away from their parents . . . even young children generally won't do that.'

At my primary school I always felt I was being singled out because I'd done something wrong. As a child of the 1960s, I was the one pulled to the front of the class to get hit on the leg or hand for my mistakes. I remember feeling a bit different, and thicker than the other kids. I have a very strong memory of being put in the hall by my head teacher; a chalk mark was made on the floor around my feet and I was told not to move. The head was very negative about me: in his view I wasn't going to amount to anything. My mum disagreed and made it clear she thought the head was talking rubbish. Having a parent looking out for that kind of singling-out in school is very important.

The impact was that I wasn't confident, always felt there was something about me that was different. I was lucky enough to pass my eleven-plus exam [which decided what type of state school pupils would attend] but I had to do it a second time – I still have atrocious writing and spelling. I assumed my difficulties – that I couldn't concentrate, made silly mistakes – were down to a lack of intelligence, but then I managed to get to medical school, because I could hyperfocus and I was interested in what I was learning.

My father almost certainly had ADHD. He would throw himself totally into something – he was an incredibly sociable and able man. He was a very successful salesman and businessman but he drowned in an accident where he was quite foolish in terms of taking appropriate safety considerations. He was very one-track.

Psychiatrist Dr Joanne Kennedy on growing up with ADHD

WHAT CAUSES ADHD?

Quick answer: we don't exactly know. However, research so far has proved that it is a highly genetic condition. Scientists have compared the rates of ADHD in identical twins (who share almost 100 per cent of the same genes) with those of fraternal twins (who share about 50 per cent of their genes). If a disorder has a genetic basis, then identical twins will be more likely to share it than fraternal twins. In 2010, researchers at Michigan State University analysing twenty-two studies of twins found a higher incidence in identical rather than fraternal twins, showing that the traits of hyperactivity and inattentiveness are heritable.

I haven't come across that many families where there is an ADHD kid and neurotypical parents and grandparents, an island of neurodivergence adrift in a neurotypical sea. (I had one hilarious encounter with an old university friend who talks nineteen to the dozen and who constantly loses her keys, misses appointments and is generally disorganised. She told me her son has ADHD and thought it came from her husband's side of the family.) It's also the case, anecdotally, that neurodivergent people find one another, fall in love and get married, often with no idea that this is the connection until later on. My husband and I used to wonder whose family the neurodivergence came from, then the answer became obvious: both. It's everywhere!

At the moment, it isn't believed to be entirely genetic, however: there is thought to be an environmental component. And yet I find that notion tricky. The idea of something in our environment being at the root of ADHD feels aligned to the theory that a brain starts off 'normal' and then something makes it 'disordered'. It doesn't gel with my dearly held belief in the fact of neurodiversity – that ADHD and autistic brains are just another flavour of brain. For my money, scientists will in future decide the factors are mostly or entirely genetic, but I've come to that view as a non-scientist so I'm prepared to be wrong and am aware that things are infinitely more complicated than the little slice of ADHD life that I perceive.

So we may not know precisely everything about what 'causes' ADHD (the question increasingly feels absurd – we don't ask what 'causes' a neurotypical brain), but we do know what *doesn't* cause it. This includes too much screen time (though the ADHD brain is likely to enthusiastically respond to screen time, for reasons we'll come on to), a poor diet (though diet can have an impact on behaviour, just as it can for anyone) and poor parenting. Ignore anyone who tells you differently. In the 1960s,

Bruno Bettelheim famously blamed autism on cold, detached 'refrigerator mothers', and while the judgement we ADHD parents receive isn't quite as overt, it's still there. Over the decades, society has come up with a conveyor belt of different reasons to blame us – mums in particular – for the fact of our children being ADHD or autistic, when really it's not a blame situation. Hopefully soon it will become just another fact, worthy of notice perhaps, but not of opprobrium, like being left-handed or green-eyed or needing glasses.

I'm personally unbothered about what the cause is and would prefer we never find out. I fear that if we do, some people will start screening for ADHD in pregnancy, and while there are undeniably some challenges associated with the condition (mostly to do with how a neurotypical society interacts with its neurodivergent population), I wouldn't take the ADHD away from my kids. Because if that happened, I'd not only lose the good parts, I'd lose *them*. Change their brain type, and in their place would be someone different. Sure, someone who might find the world easier to navigate (though neurotypicals struggle too) but also someone less funny, shrieky, precociously sweary, loving, caring, intensely sensitive, clever, loyal, considerate . . . The thought gives me shivers.

WHAT DOES ADHD FEEL LIKE?

Ping-ponging brain

I'm not on medication because I mostly like the ping-pong process in my brain. It is useful for inspiration and the velocity it brings helps me focus. The ping-pong helps me connect to my ideas, my world around me, and to people I like. But I also know that sometimes it can lead to extreme anxiety and dark thoughts and feelings of hopelessness.

Camilla Pang, author and scientist, who is AuDHD

In the diagnostic criteria of ADHD, physical hyperactivity takes centre stage because it is easy to see. What is less discussed is mental hyperactivity. Defining mental hyperactivity is tricky, as no one has done research on this subject, despite it being a constant for all ADHDers. It's possible that it's different for different people, but from what I can tell, it is essentially a constant flow of thoughts, one leading rapidly to another, in a process resembling a frenetic chain reaction of mental activity.

One poster on Reddit gives this helpful insight into their experience: 'I have a problem sometimes where I have multiple trains of thought that my mind rapid-fire switches between. So for example I'll be trying to work and my mind will rapidly switch between work, hobby one, hobby two, and music playing in the background of my mind, with random shit jokes thrown in from my mind . . . It can be extremely rapid to the point of not even finishing a thought before switching topics.'

As they say, there isn't always a chance to think thoughts through, which can make it confusing not just for the ADHD person but for the listener too, who may think: 'What is this person on about?' Someone from CAMHS once observed M in his classroom, listening to a story. When the teacher asked him a question about what happened at the end, he told her he didn't know: the story had been so boring, he'd come up with his own far more interesting ending, involving an angler fish, which he went on to describe (as the CAMHS practitioner confirmed in her notes, the teacher's story had indeed been boring).

Mental hyperactivity is pretty much about overthinking everything, all the time. There is no point telling an ADHDer not to overthink a situation: unless they are perhaps on medication, there is no other way for them to think about it. This can lead to obsessive rumination – a 'loop of doom', as I term my own personal battles with this. Studies indicate that a significant proportion of young ADHDers (up to 30 per cent) also have obsessive compulsive disorder (OCD), which is a condition where a person experiences recurring thoughts, obsessions and compulsions.

It's exhausting however you look at it and another reason why it's important to focus on a child's energy management (more information in Chapter 8). It is a good idea to talk to your child about their ping-ponging brain – for example, 'It's hard when you're expected to listen when you've got so many thoughts in your head, isn't it?' – not least so they understand this isn't something everyone has to juggle. That way they'll go easy on themselves when they aren't able to listen, or they miss information in school.

This stream of thoughts is something that doesn't change when you become an ADHD adult. Jess Wilson, an ADHDer who is a mentor at MindJam, a company that provides gaming-based mentoring to neurodivergent kids, explains.

'I was in an online lecture on Zoom recently and I didn't have a fidget close by,' she says. 'My attention was wandering. I looked up, and all of a sudden, I was like, "I really don't like my ceiling. And I don't like that ceiling light." The next thing I was googling "How can I take out a ceiling light?" and then I was looking up "How to change wiring" and "Can you change ceiling lights without having to pay an electrician?" And then I was googling ceiling lights to buy. And then the lecturer was like, "Okay, everyone, it's time for group work." And I'm like, "Oh my God! What was he talking about?"'

She also points out that even as an adult, she felt a spike of anxiety. What is it like for children at school who are experiencing a feeling of not knowing what they're meant to be doing and not being allowed to ask – again – leaving them desperately peering into other children's books for clues?

Mental hyperactivity is similar to physical hyperactivity, 'but it manifests itself in the form of chatting and a stream of thoughts constantly happening inside a person's head', says Dr Honey. 'Some hyperactive children talk all the time, like my own son. It was like having the radio on: we called it James FM. And there's the constant thinking – they can't stop their minds whirring.'

Not wanting to be alone with your thoughts

It is not uncommon for ADHDers to avoid alone time. This may be because they fear losing that external stimulation, the dopamine hit that other people deliver (no matter how exhausting they can be) – it's literally a downer being by yourself. But it can also be a fear of the unpleasant thoughts, worrying or negative overthinking that can proliferate when you're on your own. This post on Reddit sums it up: 'Every time I cook, clean or even take a shower, I have to watch something or maybe listen to some music at least. My mind just starts creating scenarios or daydreams. Then I get anxiety. Is it normal? What do you guys do? What do you think while doing chores? I'm so scared of being alone with my own thoughts.'

I can relate to this: I would never, ever opt to go for a walk on my own – the very thought gives me a spike of anxiety. Now that I have a pair of earbuds and my choice of podcasts, life is much easier. Walking back home from the bus or train after work or a night out, I sometimes call my husband and invent reasons why it's vital we talk for the ten minutes it takes to reach my front door. Sometimes he indulges me; other times he asks: 'Are you just calling me because you can't be alone?' My elder son is the same: he calls me as he leaves school each day and we speak, or don't speak, until he gets home.

Racing thoughts are, to my mind, another reason why screens are so attractive to this neurotype. It isn't just a dopamine hit; it's an off button for your ping-ponging brain. Audiobooks are magic for the same reason. Need to do a boring chore? Put on a podcast or audiobook while you do it. Company *and* something else to stimulate a brain that doesn't like doing one thing at a time. As my *Brooklyn Nine-Nine*-obsessed boys would say: bingpot!

Boring task? No chance of focus

Dr William Dodson, a psychiatrist who was one of the first practitioners to specialise in adults with ADHD, twenty-five years ago, came up with the notion of an 'interest-based nervous system', which nailed why ADHDers can focus in some environments but not in others. Basically: ADHDers need there to be interest, novelty or urgency to fire up the dopamine (more on this later) and allow them to easily pay attention. Without this they will be battling with their brain and often losing.

In an article for *ADDitude* magazine, he elaborates: 'People with ADHD primarily get in the zone by being interested in, or intrigued by, what they are doing. I call it an interest-based nervous system. Judgmental friends and family see this as being unreliable or self-serving. When friends say, "You can do the things you like", they are describing the essence of the ADHD nervous system. ADHD individuals also get in the zone when they are challenged or thrown into a competitive environment. Sometimes a new or novel task attracts their attention. Novelty is short-lived, though, and everything gets old after a while.'

He adds that most people with ADHD heavily rely upon urgency and a do-or-die deadline to get engaged in a task, and this is why procrastination is an almost universal impairment in ADHDers. The work doesn't get started until the task becomes interesting, challenging, novel or urgent (the last point means that often ADHD young people and adults rely on being stressed as a method to concentrate: what this looks like is messing around for an hour while you are meant to be doing your homework, then only getting your brain into gear once a parent gets cross or panic sets in).

For people with a neurotypical nervous system, Dodson adds, being interested in the task, or challenged, or finding the task novel or urgent is helpful, but not a prerequisite. Neurotypical people on the whole don't have to be personally interested in a task themselves – it will get done if it has 'secondary importance' too – i.e., they are motivated by the fact that their parents, teacher, boss or someone they respect thinks the task is import-ant. They will also be motivated by a reward or punishment.

But these motivations don't work for many ADHDers. In fact 'the things that motivate the rest of the world are merely nags', adds Dr Dodson.

Extreme sensitivity to rejection

Dr Dodson also coined the term rejection sensitive dysphoria (RSD), in 2017. 'Nearly everyone with ADHD answers an em-phatic yes to the question: "Have you always been more sensitive than others to rejection, teasing, criticism, or your own percep-tion that you have failed or fallen short?" This is the definition of RSD,' he explained to me.

Although it isn't an official diagnosis, clinicians are increasingly viewing it as useful context to consider, at the very least, and many ADHDers view it as a central feature of their lives.

RSD, according to Dr Dodson, causes intense mood shifts brought about by rejection – this can include the withdrawal of love, approval or respect, teasing, criticism (no matter how constructive) and persistent self-criticism or negative self-talk prompted by a real or perceived failure.

Dr Dodson's research highlights that people with RSD often feel easily embarrassed or self-conscious and have poor self-esteem. They can fall into two camps: people-pleasers or slackers. The people-pleasers avoid rejection by striving for perfection all the time and keeping others happy at all costs. They put enormous amounts of effort into tasks and easily feel a failure if they get something minor wrong. This leads inevitably to burnout and mental health problems.

The ADHD 'slackers' of this world generally aren't slackers – they are highly anxious about falling short so they prefer not to even attempt something. Because RSD is so painful, it can result in people avoiding a lot of life so they don't have to risk facing these terrible feelings. It can lead to social isolation, not applying for jobs or risking dating.

'That rejection can be how they feel about themselves when they don't meet their own impossibly high standards,' Dr Dodson says. 'Many people with ADHD may have great ability but don't do anything with it. They are sometimes described by their teachers and parents as lazy, when in fact they are overcome by fear of failure.'

The US-based writer Jillian Enright has written about how RSD shouldn't be seen as a disorder when 'it's a rational response to actual repeated rejection'. This is carried out by peers who are frustrated at having their lessons interrupted, by teachers or parents who are annoyed by the constant interruptions and chat, by the world at large as punishment for getting neurotypical life wrong. Or it can be smaller: someone is not listening to them, or the big emotional reactions that often accompany a mini-ADHDer have pushed a friend away. We've all been there – even Mother Teresa would snap when you just want your child to brush their teeth after a long day and they are avoiding the task for the nth time because they want to tell you something urgent (which keeps moving to another urgent point . . .).

There may be a flip side to this coin, however: recognition responsive euphoria (RRE), conceptualised by Dr Edward Hallowell, which he described as a 'sister syndrome' to RSD.

'Perhaps because people who have untreated ADHD are so accustomed to making mistakes and receiving criticism, they become positively giddy when they receive positive recognition.'

He adds how powerful it is for ADHDers to have their effort and good work noticed and that while we all like positive feedback, for ADHDers it's even more valued. He recommends giving praise to an ADHDer often, but only when it is due, otherwise it 'loses all its power'. For people who have ADHD who are low on motivation and energy, and not working to their potential, one reason could be that they are not getting enough recognition.

'Once you find the right person, or better still, the right people, to give you that recognition, then you can tap into the tremendous power of Recognition Responsive Euphoria,' he adds.

While I'm not personally convinced that euphoria is an entirely pleasant emotion – as I will look at later in the book, excitement doesn't always feel pleasant – I agree 100 per cent with the notion of giving mini-ADHDers lots of praise, if only to even things up. It is frequently said that young people with ADHD receive 20,000 more negative messages by the time they are twelve compared with non-ADHD people. This figure is disputed, but the principle is accurate. There is no doubt that ADHD people must cope with a lot more telling-off, a lot more shame and peer rejection: noticing the effort, the talent, the positives – generally catching a child when they are good and focusing on this more than when they aren't – is just righting a wrong.

A brain that is all or nothing when it comes to focus

There is a scene in the 1999 sci-fi film *The Matrix* where the protagonist, Neo, a computer hacker, is in a fight with the government's Agent Smith. No one can beat Smith, with his sinisterly slim sunglasses; up until this point the people he is chasing have just run away. But then Neo decides to stop running and start kung fuing. The conditions are finally right for him to realise his potential and start pulverising Agent Smith. Neo is revealed as 'The One' that everyone has been banging on about all movie, humanity's best last hope of defeating the machines.

The state in which Neo finds himself – so totally absorbed in his kunging and fuing that he forgets to be scared and suddenly finds battling Agent Smith easy – is what ADHDers might call 'the Flow', otherwise known as hyperfocus. And when Neo is in the Flow, amazing things happen.

ADHDers have to cope with a tricky attention system: one that either doesn't kick in when needed (during large parts of school) or goes into overdrive (hyperfocus) and results in stress when they're prised away from a particular task. Brandon Ashinoff is an American psychiatry research scientist with ADHD. He travelled to Birmingham University as a doctoral researcher to study ADHD attentional differences. He describes hyperfocus in an interview with me as what happens when you have 'too much focus, or you're focused so intently that no other information gets into your brain'.

He didn't get far with his studies, for reasons that will be explained, but he did publish a paper in 2019 to mark where the research had got to. Entitled 'Hyperfocus: the forgotten frontier of attention', it pulled together what little was known or conjectured about the topic. The paper defined hyperfocus as an intense state of concentration, in which external stimuli do not appear to be consciously perceived by the hyperfocuser, or they have diminished perception of their environment (i.e., you may not be aware you need to go to the toilet or are hungry). To be hyperfocused, you not only have to find the task interesting, but it needs to have the Goldilocks ratio of challenge: enough to motivate, not so much that you give up.

I met Ashinoff on Zoom five years on from him publishing his paper. As one of the only people to have studied this area, he could hopefully tell me what happens to the brain when hyperfocus kicks in. The problem was, he explained, the research has not progressed very far and so no one knows for sure.

His personal theory is that when you are in this state of intense concentration, you are more efficient at processing different types of information. So a footballer might find themselves able to process information related to foot–eye coordination more efficiently, or if you're playing a video game, the same might happen with visual perception and finger–thumb jujitsu.

But that is just Ashinoff surmising, and it's possible that you're not better at the task at all, you just think you are. Perhaps in that intense state of concentration, the good experiences are magnified and the bad minimised. 'Potentially you make decisions quickly without as much criticism of yourself,' he says. 'We know that when people make decisions faster, they tend to be more confident in those decisions.'

Speaking more generally about ADHDers' difficulties with focus, Ashinoff explains that there may be challenges shifting between focused thinking (when you have to concentrate hard and solve a problem) and diffuse thinking (when your brain relaxes, your thoughts wander and you daydream about being far away from your keyboard, on a beach, with waves lapping . . . sorry, where was I?). This hasn't been explicitly tested, though he believes it might occur because of the difficulty coordinating functions between different parts of the brain.

'Most of the time, we ADHD people live our lives in a place where we're in this very diffuse state of attention, because we're always paying attention to everything around us and it's hard to kind of focus on things in general,' he says. 'But in the circumstances where you do manage it, you then have the opposite problem: you can't switch out of it. So you can be both distractible sometimes and too focused at other times.'

He adds: 'When I was a kid growing up, I did not like a lot of elements of school – I was very distractible and I had a lot of trouble focusing on homework – but when I got to work on a topic I cared about, I was zoned in. When the lesson didn't interest me, though, I would read books under my desk.'

As an adult, Ashinoff finds that hyperfocus helps with elements of his job. He will look up, having sat down to do a burst of programming or coding as part of his psychiatry work, to find that four hours have passed. 'It helps to set up the right environment to get into the Flow: for example, I prefer coding at the office and writing at home. Because my internet drops when I'm at home, and is slower, this breaks my focus when I'm coding. Whereas with writing it's, you know, Microsoft Word, it works anywhere. And I like my computer at home better.'

Ashinoff doesn't believe hyperfocus is a 'superpower' exclusive to the neurodivergent community, but he is interested to find out whether those who are neurodivergent are more likely to be able to slip into that state, or if there are differences in the hyperfocus experience between the neurotypes. 'It could be that ADHDers hyperfocus more frequently, or maybe we don't but the experience is more intense [than for neurotypicals]. Or it is as frequent and as intense, but it lasts longer . . . There's a lot of ways it could vary.'

His studies at Birmingham eventually stalled because it turned out it is very difficult to judge when someone is in hyperfocus. 'You can't get a person to break out of hyperfocus to tell you they're in it, because if they do, they're not any more, and that breaks your whole experiment,' he says.

'As a grad student, I spent a year trying to develop a task to induce hyperfocus. And it was a complete failure with no usable data. As I needed to graduate in a certain period of time, I switched to something easier. But since I had spent a year researching and writing, I published a paper as I didn't want it to go to waste. The whole point of my paper is to say, "Look, there's this thing that clearly happens. It seems to be this critical symptom of ADHD and it's often ignored."' And the reason it is ignored may partly be down to the fact that hyperfocus 'is the antithesis of what ADHD is historically defined as'.

Ashinoff adds: 'You do wonder why hyperfocus isn't included [in the *DSM-5* diagnostic manual] given how frequently it comes up, anecdotally. One point in there does have a flavour of hyperfocus – the *DSM-5* says that the ADHD child "often does not seem to listen when spoken to directly" – but it's not explicit and I think it should be. One likely reason it's not there is that there is no literature on it, and before something is included in the *DSM-5* they will need clear empirical data.'

Hyperfocus can be a very helpful tool in keeping ADHD children happy. If teachers had the time to think more about the quality of the tasks they set these pupils – not just tasks that (as much as possible) interest them but the right level of challenge – that would be immensely valuable. It's also useful for parents to recognise your child's interests and help create the conditions for hyperfocus. If they want to geek out on Pokémon for hours, limit the distractions. And helping children to pick subjects and specialise where they can hyperfocus as soon as possible can be beneficial too.

Having just one thing to do at a time is not enough for a busy ADHD brain

Multitasking is a myth. Women can't do it any more than men can. No one can process more than one thought at a time; instead, all of us move from one to another linearly, albeit at different speeds. So multitasking should more properly be called 'task switching'. Some people can do it more quickly than others, and ADHDers can do it very rapidly indeed. Researchers at Stanford University have measured the effect of task switching on our brains and in our lives. What they found is that it makes people less effective at work, as well as impairing their decision-making abilities. It also triggers greater stress, which negatively affects the health and social lives of those trying to juggle several things at the same time. Except for one group, that is. One group of people don't experience additional stress when they have a lot on their plate (though it does affect their productivity): ADHDers.

Both my sons, when confronted with the horror of English homework, will always try to do something, anything else at the same time. Over time, it's dawned on me why: their brains hate doing just one thing. So I now allow them to flit between tasks (though not always in very sensible ways, I confess: E sometimes combines solving quadratic equations with checking his Discord notifications). It may not be the most efficient way to get the homework done, but at least it means it's getting done.

Occupational therapists often conceptualise ADHD as the need for huge amounts of stimulation to feel right. My dad, who I think had ADHD – a thought that occurred to me only after he died so will for ever remain an untested theory – would often read a newspaper while watching TV and listening to music and seemed able to take in all the information at once. He could fulminate over the latest political shenanigans, describe every ball from the last three overs in the Test match and then discourse at length on the track playing, telling you what year and where he saw any given band play.

The disgraced businessman Sam Bankman-Fried, who was convicted of fraud and related crimes in November 2023 when he ran the crypto company FTX, was notorious for doing something like this. Bankman-Fried, who has ADHD, was said to habitually play computer games while carrying out meetings and was once caught playing the video game *League of Legends* during a meeting with investors from Sequoia Capital, the Silicon Valley venture capital giant that made billions of dollars as an early investor in Google and WhatsApp.

This meeting was reported in an illuminating piece on Sequoia's website (which has since been removed, according to the

Business Insider website), featuring a quote from Ramnik Arora, FTX's head of product. Arora described how Bankman-Fried was selling his vision to the investors. 'I sit ten feet from him, and I walked over, thinking, "Oh, shit, that was really good." And it turns out that that f-cker was playing *League of Legends* through the entire meeting.'

As a pupil, Brandon Ashinoff developed an ability to read a book and listen in class at the same time. 'If I remember correctly, I was able to read the book and still get the teacher's questions correct,' he says. 'So you could make the argument that one element of that task was autopilot, and the other element was active. I was probably splitting my attention and able to pay enough attention to try and make it look like I wasn't reading the book. It's possible I was finding a way to get my brain to engage more [during a boring lesson].'

With ADHD kids (and adults), if they aren't challenged enough, the attentional leakage becomes a bigger problem, whereas if the task at hand is sufficiently challenging, the leakage is contained and this reduces the need to do something else at the same time or attention wandering elsewhere. Again, it comes back to finding the sweet spot for the ADHD child between something being challenging enough yet not too frustrating.

TL;DR (TOO LONG; DIDN'T READ)

A summary for those with shorter attention spans (and no judgement here).

- Ask for an assessment for ADHD at the early stages of thinking about it – don't leave it too late.
- Be aware of inattentive ADHD – a child who is disengaged, dreamy – which is less understood than the hyperactive/ impulsive presentation.

- ADHD isn't caused by poor parenting, poor diet or too much screen time.
- Having a 'ping-ponging' busy brain can be brilliant for ideas but can also mean overthinking and obsessive rumination.
- ADHD people genuinely find it very hard to focus on a task that is boring; their brain doesn't consistently have enough dopamine, so they rely on interest/novelty/urgency to fire up the neurotransmitter.
- Don't tease an ADHDer! Extreme sensitivity to rejection is part and parcel of this neurotype – even if the rejection is perceived and not real.
- On the upside there is hyperfocus, which is a bit of ADHD magic. This allows a person to concentrate on a topic and bypass what are usual human functions while that person focuses.
- ADHD people can't do two things at once (no one can), but they can flit between tasks quicker and with less stress.
- When ADHD brains don't have enough to interest them there can be 'attentional leakage'. Creating the Goldilocks zone of focus – enough interest and challenge – is the key to satisfying an ADHD brain.

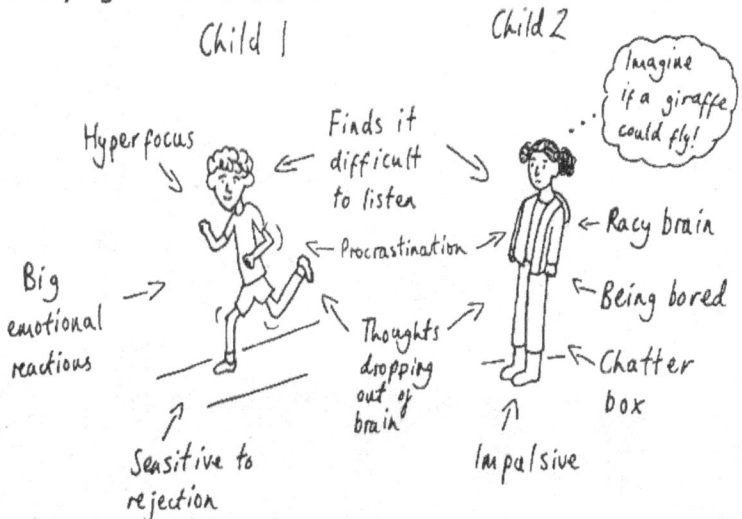

4

The Diagnosis Process

People who feel ADHD is overdiagnosed sometimes express the view that modern life is obsessed with labels. As a label enthusiast, I see this as no bad thing. Which is just as well, as my children have many of them – my elder son has three so far (ADHD, ASC – autism spectrum condition – and DCD, which stands for developmental coordination disorder and which used to be known as dyspraxia) and my younger has four, with persistent desire for autonomy (formerly known as pathological demand avoidance) added to the mix too. The neurodiversity box set, you might say.

I've always been pro labels, but my experiences with my younger son have left me more so than ever. We started properly thinking he might have ADHD when he was about five, but he didn't get a diagnosis until he was eight. Three years may not seem such a long time, but in that time everything went wrong. His self-esteem plummeted, his anxiety soared and he could no longer cope with school.

Part of the problem was the lack of a label, which is a definitive answer. Obviously, you can support your child without one, but there will always be that nagging thought in your head questioning if you are right or not, which can undermine any resolve or plans you have. It also makes it harder to speak to school and teachers confidently about what needs to be done.

But even I notice a tinge of embarrassment sometimes when I tell people my children are AuDHD and the rest. 'I didn't realise your child had ADHD *as well as* autism,' some people have said, which makes me want to ask in return: how many labels are we allowed – just the one?

While I'm not in any way ashamed of my boys, I do sometimes worry that the people I'm talking to will disbelieve their diagnoses. And that would feel as if people were disbelieving who my sons *are*, given that their ADHD and autism are part of their identity. That we, their parents, have got everything wrong.

While I've been writing this book, a barrage of opinion columns and news pieces have been published that reflect the view that the increase in the number of ADHD diagnoses is a form of social contagion fuelled by TikTok videos and the desire for a label to explain away normal life problems. It has, depressingly, been dragged into the culture wars.

There is an assumption that we are in the midst of an over-diagnosis pandemic, fuelled by private doctors paid by over-anxious parents. But there is no evidence to say there is overdiagnosis happening, let alone that it's widespread. In fact, it is more likely that we have an underdiagnosis crisis, as the Australian journalist Matilda Boseley neatly argues in her book *The Year I Met My Brain*.

Boseley explains that because the number of people diagnosed with ADHD isn't the same as the number of people who actually have it (since not everyone knows they have ADHD), it is best to work out how common it is by looking at studies that take a random group of people and screen them all. These 'meta-analysis studies', which look at hundreds of thousands of data points around the world, have found that the average proportion of children and teenagers with ADHD worldwide is between 5.9 and 7.2 per cent.

If we look at UK rates, the most accurate sources are likely to be *The Lancet*, one of the oldest peer-reviewed medical journals in the world, and the NHS watchdog the National Institute for Health and Care Excellence (NICE). They suggest that about 5 per cent of children and teens have ADHD. This suggests a significant pattern of underdiagnosis in this country, by between 0.9 and 2.2 percentage points. Given that there are just over 14 million people under the age of eighteen in the UK, this would mean that around 700,000 currently are diagnosed with ADHD but between 127,000 and 310,000 more children have it but are going under the radar.

As Boseley points out, the only country that comes close to exceeding the global prevalence estimates is the US and then only in some states. In South Korea, just 0.04 per cent of the population gets a diagnosis.

I'm not arguing that misdiagnosis never happens – of course it does, especially as there are lots of features of ADHD that overlap with other conditions, such as OCD and some trauma characteristics – but the data above suggests that the problem we should be talking about in the UK is not the fact that children are being wrongly identified as having ADHD but that so many of them are not being identified at all.

Given the backdrop, it's no surprise that we feel awkward when we tell friends and family our kids are being assessed for ADHD. If you fear absolutely no judgement, then you are either unusually brave or capable of not caring whatsoever – in which case I salute you! Watch out if you do feel that twinge of embarrassment, though. Kick against it. That shame you feel is the weight of society bearing down, telling you, with no evidence, that there is a correct level of diagnoses, and we've passed it. It makes it harder to feel justified in seeking a diagnosis.

No doubt society felt the same when people started coming out as gay, the first brave souls inspiring and encouraging others to do the same. Cue the backlash, the anger, the pearl-clutching and questions over what was causing this explosion in perceived 'deviancy', which is simply a deviation from the norm. Then, after far too much time had passed, the majority finally realised it wasn't that numbers were rocketing, there was no proliferation of gayness; it was just that being gay wasn't as rare – or as terrible – as they initially thought. And what's more, there was no need to try to keep a lid on numbers by making it as difficult as possible for people to come out.

The only thing ill-informed discussion will do is delay diagnoses in the short term as families struggle to overcome the social stigma and make that first call to their GP. They often then have to sit for years on an NHS waiting list because the people in charge have not put adequate resources in place to assess their child.

I now think I allowed the people talking about overdiagnosis to get in my head, and this played a part in delaying recognition of what was happening. If I had my time again, I would mentally tell those people to fuck off and would just go straight to the GP. If we were a purely logical society, we'd see the increase in diagnoses – for a condition that can have appalling mental health outcomes if people are left in the dark and for which access to medication can reduce the likelihood of the most distressing mental health problems – as a reason to celebrate.

BEFORE THE DIAGNOSIS

You think your child needs to be assessed – what do you do

Speak to your nursery or school SENCO (special educational needs coordinator – every school has to have one) and ask them to make a referral to your local NHS CAMHS, which is in charge of assessing for ADHD. This is what happened with us, but if the school doesn't want to do this – perhaps because it's another long form they have to fill in and they're too busy – ask your GP to refer. Go to your local surgery prepared to explain why you think your child needs an assessment: that they have attention differences that are not in line with their peers, for example, or they need a lot more regulating activities to feel settled; they have difficulties with organising themselves – packing their school bag or tidying up after themselves in class; they find it hard not to interrupt and/or are having social difficulties.

Once the referral has been made, it's probably wise to get in touch with CAMHS to check they have received it and to make a note of the date so you have a record. If you can, it's helpful to get to know someone at CAMHS and develop a relationship with them so you can ask questions and be the person they think of if a last-minute appointment magically appears. Sometimes people mysteriously drop off waiting lists, so keep checking in.

While you wait . . . and wait . . .

At the time of writing, some families are reporting that it takes three years just to get on the waiting list.

We got lucky in that CAMHS assigned us a caseworker, who visited our son, clocked that he was likely to get a diagnosis and liaised with us and school to set up some support while we waited. Her view was that he wasn't okay at school and was masking. Initially I resisted this idea: I felt I would know if he was masking and didn't even know ADHD children did this. It took perhaps a year or two to realise she was exactly right. In retrospect I feel that in the early days I resisted what professionals were telling me, assuming I knew best because he was my child and I would have known if he was struggling. But I didn't and now wish I'd kept more of an open mind.

While you're there twiddling your thumbs, it's a good idea to keep a diary of what is working for your child and what isn't. This will not only become helpful evidence when your child finally gets their assessment but will also allow you to support them better in the meantime. Notice what triggers meltdowns and write it down. What makes your child happy and relaxed? What makes them anxious and dysregulated? What activities help them be more regulated? What helps them focus – an audiobook? Music? Fidgets? What type? You'll get RSI from mouse-clicking and be one of Amazon's most treasured customers by the time you've found your child's fidget match. Keeping a record means you can spot patterns. It also means you can do less of what stresses your child out and more of what makes them happy and allows them to focus.

You could also start a Google Doc of observations for when the assessment finally happens, somewhere to store things the school has said that could be useful for the clinicians undertaking the assessment. Some parents take videos of their child to document their high energy at home or them coming out of school dysregulated. This can be helpful but needs to be carefully done so it's not too weird for the child. Don't film them in distress – while it's understandable to want professionals to see how bad it can get, seeing you behind the camera phone rather than supporting them will only add to their upset.

If there is good reason to think your child will end up with a diagnosis, check with the school that they are registered as being under SEN (special educational needs) Support, which means you will have termly meetings about available help. If you're not sure if you will end up with a diagnosis but your child is struggling, your school can and should put in place support anyway (see Chapter 10: Support at School for more info).

If things are getting bad, involve CAMHS and send them regular updates. See if you can be allocated a caseworker while you wait, and if you are, keep in touch with them – ask them which professionals can be involved to support your child and the school. Keep the updates factual and try not to get cross about the waiting list – they are likely to be just as despairing as you are about it.

In the end, we went private, as things were getting bad at school and we needed a clear diagnosis. Of course, it was sod's law that just after the private assessment we found out we'd got to the top of the NHS waiting list.

Right to choose

Under the 'right to choose' scheme, it can be possible to get an NHS referral to a private service if the wait for the local NHS service is very long. Speak to your GP about it, as the referral starts with them. The GP will need to agree there is a clinical need, so offer clear reasons for requesting it. There is information on the NHS and ADHD UK websites about this.

From what age can a child be diagnosed?

According to the NICE guidelines, ADHD assessment and diagnosis can begin from the age of four. This is meant to involve observation of the child's behaviour across different settings – home and school – though in these days of huge waiting lists, it is now often based on how a child is observed just in the clinic. Teachers will be asked to fill in forms, and while some weight is attached to their views – they are in a great position to spot differences – it is also true that not all teachers are knowledgeable about or any good at spotting the signs of ADHD, and clinicians, based on my conversations with them at any rate, are aware of this.

Sometimes people get fobbed off by being told it is not their local authority's policy to assess children below, say, the age of eight. But my advice is to not pay any attention to these local policies and be firm that your child needs to be assessed sooner. My son was eight when he got diagnosed and it was too late as we'd hit crisis by that point.

For younger children (under the age of six) it can be more challenging to diagnose ADHD because symptoms of inattention, hyperactivity and impulsivity are common among this age group. Professionals are therefore likely to take a more cautious approach, often involving multiple assessments over time to confirm the diagnosis, though they may give parents an indication that they feel support needs to be put in place in school while a child waits.

THE DIAGNOSIS

Who makes the diagnosis and what does it involve?

The diagnosis is usually made by a psychiatrist. When they assess your child, they will ask questions about their early development, observe them and use standardised questionnaires. Wherever possible there will be consideration of the child's view and any challenges they have in daily life.

On the day

I don't remember much of M's assessment (which was only two years ago) and I don't know why I can't recall more about it. Is it because I was stressed? Or too relaxed? I know I didn't much like the psychiatrist's manner, who I felt spent the bare minimum of time explaining anything to us. I also didn't do any of the things below, so bear in mind this advice is coming from a flawed parent who doesn't always put into practice what she tells you to do.

What I do know is that what you, the parent, observe is very important evidence, so it's a good idea to gather your thoughts and notes so you can be articulate and precise, giving concrete examples where possible. Does it take, say, five minutes before your child loses focus or gets fidgety if they are doing something they aren't interested in? But they can look at their Pokémon cards or play Dungeons & Dragons for four hours straight? What happens when you ask them to pack their school bag? (Observe your child without intervening and write down what happens.) Do they need tasks to be broken down into smaller chunks? Do they zone out frequently, seem mentally very busy? Do they come home from school in an angry mood and tear around the house amped up? What helps them calm down?

Consider emailing a summary of your behaviour diary to the psychiatrist before the appointment, perhaps with a list of what your child is good at and what they find difficult, as well as any videos you have taken. Take a list of questions to the assessment so you don't forget to ask anything. 'The people who know kids best are parents,' says Dr Joanne Kennedy, consultant psychiatrist at Stepping Stones Clinic and a veteran CAMHS psychiatrist at several local authorities. 'I always find that kids mask so much – the teachers may say everything is fine but the parents know and the kids themselves know.'

What your doctor is looking for

The key diagnostic criteria for ADHD as outlined in the *DSM-5* and quoted below are divided into three presentations: predominantly inattentive, predominantly hyperactive-impulsive and combined.

Predominantly inattentive presentation. At least six (or five for those seventeen years and older) of the following symptoms of inattention must be present for at least six months and are inappropriate for the developmental level:

- Often fails to give close attention to details, or makes careless mistakes in schoolwork, work or other activities.

- Often has difficulty sustaining attention in tasks or play activities.
- Often does not seem to listen when spoken to directly.
- Often does not follow through on instructions and fails to finish schoolwork, chores or duties in the workplace (not due to oppositional behaviour or failure to understand instructions).
- Often has difficulty organising tasks and activities.
- Often avoids, dislikes or is reluctant to engage in tasks that require sustained mental effort (such as schoolwork or homework).
- Often loses things necessary for tasks or activities (e.g. toys, school assignments, pencils, books or tools).
- Is often easily distracted by extraneous stimuli.
- Is often forgetful in daily activities.

Predominantly hyperactive-impulsive presentation. At least six (or five for those seventeen years and older) of the following symptoms of hyperactivity-impulsivity must be present for at least six months and are inappropriate for the developmental level:

- Often fidgets with or taps hands or feet or squirms in seat.
- Often leaves seat in situations when remaining seated is expected.
- Often runs about or climbs in situations where it is inappropriate (adolescents or adults may be limited to feeling restless).
- Often unable to play or engage in leisure activities quietly.
- Is often 'on the go', acting as if 'driven by a motor'.
- Often talks excessively.
- Often blurts out answers before questions have been completed.
- Often has difficulty waiting their turn.
- Often interrupts or intrudes on others (e.g. butts into conversations or games).

Combined presentation. This is diagnosed when both criteria for inattention and hyperactivity-impulsivity are met for the past six months. Additional criteria:

- Symptoms present before age twelve: several symptoms must have been present before age twelve.
- Symptoms in two or more settings: several symptoms must be present in two or more settings (e.g. at home, school or work; with friends or relatives; in other activities).
- Clear evidence of interference: there must be clear evidence that the symptoms interfere with or reduce the quality of social, school or work functioning.
- Not better explained by another disorder: the symptoms do not occur exclusively during the course of schizophrenia or another psychotic disorder and are not better explained by another mental disorder (e.g. mood disorder, anxiety disorder, dissociative disorder, personality disorder, substance intoxication or withdrawal).

The diagnosis report

A diagnosis report usually follows a few weeks later. It should be detailed, stating your concerns, giving a history of your child's development, the clinician's observations, a diagnostic conclusion and recommendations for what future support your child is likely to need. It should also include which methods were used to reach the diagnosis.

If you're not happy, raise any points you don't agree with or areas you feel are missing. You want the report to be helpful for the school and for any future requests for support, so it's sensible to make sure it's detailed in its recommendations. The clinician needs to be specific if they can be – and if they haven't been, ask why the report can't be more precise, otherwise the local authority won't accept the diagnosis and getting support may be trickier.

The report may include medical jargon that you don't understand, in which case you can email the doctor to clarify. Wading through several pages about your child's difficulties can be tough, but these points need to be in there in order to access the right support.

Some clinicians will do a separate report for your child in language they can understand, setting out the diagnosis and what it means (though if they just list a set of so-called impairments, chuck it in the recycling bin!). Having someone who is not their parent or carer telling them their trouble focusing has nothing to do with their effort or intelligence – and that they are not naughty if they find it hard to be still or not blurt things out or interrupt – may be immensely helpful to a child's self-esteem.

AFTER THE DIAGNOSIS . . .

For most parents, what follows is a process of soul-searching and information-gathering. I was surprised how much I was affected by M's diagnoses. I had been through it all once before with E, and thought by the second time round it would involve less worry and guilt, but it didn't. It is impossible not to have an emotional reaction when your child's difficulties are being laid out before you and you are being given an early heads-up on some things that will always be a challenge for them, as a child and an adult.

I felt guilty because I had been too busy with work to notice how difficult things were getting for him. And perhaps I was too wedded to the idea that he was happy. After a complicated few early years with my elder son, we were so determined to have a happy younger child (proof perhaps that our parenting was up to scratch, the kind of reassurance you don't often get as the parent of a neurodivergent child) that we held on to this notion tightly, right up until the point the medical professionals gently prised it out of our grasp. We needed to face up to the complicated reality that while our boy appeared on the surface and to the untrained eye to be a chatty, confident extrovert, a charmer and a joke-cracker, the reality was more complicated.

Telling your child

We've always talked about ADHD and autism since M was young, so for him there was no big reveal. He was the one who identified he had ADHD, after all, at that fateful school assembly at the age of five – he just had to wait far too long for it to be confirmed three years later.

The idea of being an ADHDer was a welcome one at first (though later his relationship with ADHD got more complicated). I'd gone through this big realisation writing my first book that being neurotypical is not the goal, and clearly I managed to communicate this message very effectively to my two sons. I remember one morning, when M was about four, we were sitting at the breakfast table and he asked us if he was autistic like his brother. We said no (which turned out to be wrong) and he burst into tears. After consoling him, I remember feeling very amused that in our household being neurotypical was the undesirable outcome.

Not everyone sees it this way, of course. A teacher friend told me that she went to a talk on ADHD attended by SENCOs, the teachers charged with overseeing support for SEND kids in a school. Some SENCOS at private schools spoke about how parents were refusing to send them copies of their child's assessment report, because they didn't want the ADHD diagnosis to be on their record. Once the child was on medication, the parents didn't want the term ADHD to be attached to them again.

This is a deeply awful message to send: that part of their identity is shameful. That they've been born wrong, have been medicated to make them right. That no one else – teachers, school, parents – has to change.

On the flip side, I'm friends with a mum of a boy who thinks he has ADHD. After we chatted about this, she told me matter-of-factly that her son is perfect as he is, so 'the world is just going to have to change around him'. I loved this take: for too long we've expected neurodivergent children to do all the changing; now it's society's turn. (As it turns out, her son, who is M's best pal, does happen to be perfect. Thoughtful, clever, with social insights that take my breath away, a wonderful and caring friend – and clearly ADHD.)

I'm a believer in being honest and talking to your child about everything, all the way through the assessment process. If your instinct is not to, ask yourself why. Is there some part of you that sees ADHD negatively, having grown up absorbing all the nonsense, untruths and stigma?

I've known very well-meaning people not to tell their children of their diagnoses and I strongly feel this is wrong. The diagnosis is a crucial piece of information, and if you don't give your child a label, they or their peers will inevitably find a worse one. Stupid, shit at life, clumsy, away with the fairies, weird, annoying, naughty. Not knowing who you are and why you find some things difficult, if not impossible, when everyone else seems to find them easy is a difficult place to be. A label also allows a child to go easy on themselves for things linked to their neurotype, like difficulties with organisation; the chance to advocate for themselves if the environment is wrong for them. All these things, crucial for happiness, you lose without an explanation. A child without knowledge of who they are is likely to mask more. About half of ADHD adults have an anxiety disorder, and masking is one reason why mental health outcomes for adults are as terrible as they are. In an ideal world, where there was equal respect and opportunities and allowances for all the different brain types, we wouldn't need labels, but until then we do.

WHAT OTHER CONDITIONS MIGHT YOUR CHILD HAVE?

Learning difficulty and learning disability

People with a learning disability tend to take longer to learn and may need support to develop new skills, understand complicated information and interact with other people, according to Mencap, a UK charity for people with a learning disability. The level of support someone needs depends on the individual, and there are some very able people with learning disabilities who lead fulfilling lives but may need support getting a job or living independently. Someone more disabled may need full-time care and support in every aspect of their life. A learning difficulty is not related to intellectual ability but to learning – that is, how knowledge is gained and processed. Learning difficulties are very common in ADHD children and the label can be applied when there is a discrepancy between achievement and intellectual ability. Part of an educational psychologist's role is to identify learning difficulties and advise the school on strategies to remove the barriers to learning.

Autism

It is hard to write what autism is in a few paragraphs, and for some stellar information on the subject – perhaps if your child is autistic too, and there is quite a high chance they will be – you could do worse than read a great book, *Autism: How to Raise a Happy Autistic Child*, which also happens to be written by me.

Autism generally is the yin to ADHD's yang: the autistic child will have a clear need for predictability and structure, which is opposite to ADHDers' need for newness and difficulties with organisation and therefore structuring their lives. An autistic child typically finds navigating the social jungle of school confusing, stressful and exhausting. Anxiety is likely to be a constant companion, and an autistic child may have big difficulties knowing what emotions they are feeling, let alone labelling and discussing them. They may also find it difficult to intuitively read what someone else is feeling, though they are likely to care very much once they are told.

They may also have phenomenal skills in the area they are interested in, be very talented at spotting patterns, develop enormous skills in an area linked to an interest and – despite what the stereotypes say – be hyper-empathetic, hoovering up the vibe of the room.

But most of all, autistic people prefer to be allowed to be monotropic: to wallow in their attention tunnel and not be pulled too much from it by conversation or parents or teachers. They may find unstructured chat, with its lack of rules and parameters, annoying and stressful.

They are also afflicted with sensory overload. To empathise with this, imagine that all your senses are more intense. The hum of your dishwasher is louder, the overhead lights brighter, your jumper itchier. It's distracting while you're trying to work, it's draining to pretend it isn't bothering you, and you become increasingly stressed as a result. Or you may not realise it's stressing you out, but for some reason you arrive home exhausted and tearful nearly every day.

AuDHD

Nowadays you can be diagnosed as both autistic and ADHD – and there is a growing community of AuDHDers who are forging a separate identity and sharing their experience of having both. Up until recently, the two conditions were considered mutually exclusive, with the *DSM* stating that the diagnosis of one precluded the existence of the other. This was revised in the 2013 edition.

Now some specialists believe that the coexistence of the two conditions is not just possible, but frequent. One study by researchers at Duke University found that up to half of people diagnosed as autistic also exhibit ADHD symptoms, and that characteristics of autism are present in two thirds of people with ADHD. Dr Jessica Eccles, the chairwoman of the Royal College of Psychiatrists' neurodevelopmental special interest group, says that in her clinical experience, it's more than three quarters.

'I spent ages trying to figure out if I was one or the other, and then it was like, "Oh, it turns out I'm both – no wonder that was so hard to decide",' says Kirstie McStay, community manager at Spectrum Gaming. Having both is complicated, as the two neuro-types can work in opposition. McStay adds: 'The autistic side of me wants deliberative decision-making – to absorb all the information possible about something before acting upon it – but the ADHD side wants to be more spontaneous without thinking too hard, and that desire to "shortcut" the decision-making can be stressful.'

The tension between the two conditions can be exhausting, but there can also be significant upsides. Creativity is frequently cited as a benefit, and the novelty and lateral thoughts of ADHD combined with the autism focus can lead to amazing things. A report written by the academic Mike Connor published in February 2013, entitled 'Differentiating Autism Spectrum Disorder and Attention Deficit Disorder', concluded that the presence of ADHD symptoms in autistic children might actually lead to more social interaction, as a result of increased talkativeness. But it's also true that the paradoxes of AuDHD can camouflage each other, or even – on the surface at least – cancel each other out, which is why some AuDHDers experience missed or incorrect diagnoses.

Fergus Murray, whose mother was the late Dinah Murray, the woman behind the monotropism theory, is a science teacher and writer, and believes that monotropism – the desire to focus on one thing and not have your attention moved unnecessarily – may be the unifying force between ADHD and autism. They themselves are AuDHD, and point out in an article they wrote for their Monotropism.org website, along with their partner, the therapist Sonny Hallett, that ADHD and autism are characterised in the diagnostic manuals in completely different ways. So the fact that so many people have both might seem initially surprising.

'It cries out for an explanation,' they write. 'One possibility is that autism and ADHD share an underlying cause. Monotropism has been put forward as one candidate for this.'

Pathological demand avoidance

Pathological demand avoidance (PDA) was first identified by the late developmental psychologist Elizabeth Newson and applies to autistic children who can find it difficult, if not frankly intolerable, to manage what others view as simple demands and requests. If pressed to comply, they may fly into a rage or have a meltdown, a response that presents as angry behaviour though it is in fact driven by chronic anxiety. I've included PDA (more recently reframed as persistent drive for autonomy) here because early research suggests it occurs in AuDHD children. In the past, it has been seen as a subset of autistic experience but is now being seen as a normal part of being autistic or AuDHD, with people experiencing it to a greater or lesser extent depending on their stress levels. If a child is struggling to cope in a large, busy school, for example, feeling out of control, with their body in flight-or-fight mode most of the time, demand avoidance – school refusal, meltdowns, unwillingness to get dressed, eat, brush hair or teeth – is a pretty understandable response to establish control of the situation.

PDA isn't currently recognised by the *DSM*, nor is there a standardised test for it. The Elizabeth Newson Centre in Nottingham is the country's leading diagnostic centre. Currently we are in a weird position where some parts of the NHS seem to recognise it unofficially, but not others. As it's not an official diagnosis given out by the NHS, some practitioners get round this by diagnosing autism with a 'demand avoidant' profile – which was M's diagnosis. In hindsight, it wasn't in any doubt: it probably sealed the deal when he continually walked out of the room because the psychologist was trying to get him to read something. 'I didn't come out of school for you to give me more school!' he memorably said at one point. I laughed out loud and felt immense pride reading that bit of the report – that's my boy.

M is now nine and, like a large number of kids who share the same presentation, is out of school – it's been nine months now (more on this later). When he was little, during one of the many blazing rows we had, going head-to-head because I wanted him to do something and he couldn't cope with it, he said to me, 'I don't know why I can't say yes.' What he meant was he was finding it impossible to say yes, even though he knew what was expected of him and wanted to comply. You can imagine the implications for school of this overwhelming desire for autonomy. Educating a class of thirty-plus is as much about crowd control as imparting information, and it's understandable that teachers expect pupils to do as they're told and have limited time to argue the toss.

The only effective way to approach demand avoidance is to reduce demands and rephrase them as requests or as a statement – rather than telling your child, 'Put on your shoes,' you might say: 'I've left your shoes by the door.'

An additional factor is that the PDA child may not perceive the social hierarchy of age and authority that we grew up with. They see themselves as being on the same level as their parents and teachers, and want a relationship of equals. Being told what to do, or not being in control, will cause them huge problems, as their nervous system is telling their brain to interpret the demand as a threat.

Having a child with these challenges has at times been intensely complicated for all of us. It challenges all your trad-itional notions of parenting: rather than you telling them what to do and expecting it to happen, you have to get used to a more collaborative approach. It's about getting them onside, encour-aging them, and often – most helpfully – simply levelling with them, explaining the reasons you want them to do something. Yes, it's time-consuming, but it has taught me to be far more patient, to listen better and to afford M the same respect I would for someone else's child.

What I have found most helpful during those times when I feel myself transforming into My Way or the Highway Mum is to remember that this is about him rather than me. His needs and happiness are more important than the delicious and lovingly prepared dinner I've made for him to be eaten hot, for example. Because I know that if I give in to my urge to tell him to get off *Minecraft* this second because his food is on the table – rather than, say, asking him when this particular bit of the game will end – the result will be an argument or a meltdown. And after the meltdown comes the self-hatred and the guilt, so he ends up feeling even shitter about himself than he already does. That's something you need to keep in check.

Don't listen to anyone who tells you that being strict will solve the problem. It won't. It will make things far worse. So if your child is refusing to come to the table, wait a bit longer, stick their dinner in the fridge until they're ready, or – look away, 1970s parents! – bring it to them in their bedroom. And if they're refusing to go to school, explain to the teachers that they aren't being naughty; it is anxiety driving the avoidance, a condition that is associated with high levels of masking. What your child needs at school is flexibility and to feel understood. The goal should be to lower the demands placed upon them, and thus lower their anxiety and make them feel emotionally stronger. Once you've achieved this, you can try to gradually introduce boundaries again, in a spirit of collaboration and open discussion about what's hard and what's possible.

There's so much more to be said about PDA, but perhaps that's something for another book. In the meantime, visit the website of the PDA Society, which has the best advice out there, and watch the videos of Casey Ehrlich (a PDA parent coach) and Naomi Fisher (a clinical psychologist) on YouTube. Keep an open mind and involve your child in the solution. A sentence I sometimes use is: 'I'm worried this situation is going to lead us to arguing and I really don't want that – what do you think we should do?' And recognise that, however challenging PDA can be for a parent, it's harder for the child.

Being open about these difficulties – discussing with your child that they can have a large reaction to being told what to do, and it's not their fault, but we need to work out strategies to make life easier – can only make relationships better, which means we must give our children the language and understanding to do so. Bear this in mind: it's usually not that your child won't do something, it's that they can't.

Kirsti Hadley is AuDHD and demand-avoidant. She sometimes has to trick her brain to get things done. 'The more you realise something is important for you to do, and it's going to be a pain if you don't do it, the less you're able to do it as it becomes a demand,' she says. Hadley has advised other parents on strategies for working with demand avoidance. Her advice is to name it and talk about it.

'A friend's son used to like using the hairdryer at night in bed for long periods of time – he was blasting it over his body. He liked the heat and the white noise, but obviously he can't do it for too long as that's a bit of a fire hazard. One night, after half an hour of using the hairdryer, my friend said, "It's really time to turn that hairdryer off now." Now, she normally knows better than to say it directly but she was tired. And she told me her son just looked at her and went, "Oh, Mom, I was just about to switch off, and now you've told me to, you know I can't!" So she said, "What do you want to do then? How are we going to fix this?" Her son said, "Well, I'm going to dry myself for five more minutes and then I'm going to give it to you, and then you can dry my back. But then you've got to give it back to me and I will switch it off." You find a different way around things that just must look mad to anybody from the outside.'

Hopefully you will now have a better understanding of the diagnosis process, and the likelihood of your child having another neurotype too. While hearing (or reading) about your child's difficulties is never going to be easy, look at it as a one-sided view of your child's differences that is far from the whole picture. For your child it may be confirmation that they aren't wrong, stupid or lazy – they just process information differently. Diagnosis can mean your child can find their tribe, or learn who they really are. For this to happen early on in life – rather than having to figure out who you really are in middle age – is an incredible gift.

TL;DR

A quick summary of what we've discussed above.

- While you wait for an assessment, keep a Google Doc of things you notice about your child that might be relevant: what stresses them out, what calms them down, what challenges they have in school, social difficulties, etc.
- According to NICE guidelines, a child can be assessed from the age of four, ignore people who tell you to wait.
- Your child can be diagnosed with hyperactive/impulsive ADHD (which does what it says on the tin); inattentive ADHD (when a child is more dreamy/disengaged); or combined (when they are both of these things).

- Recent research has suggested up to half of ADHD people are also autistic, though some academics are suggesting it's more like three-quarters.
- Kids who are AuDHD may have a strong drive to be in control too. Persistent drive for autonomy (PDA) can make life very difficult in school, and needs the school to adopt specific learning strategies.
- Some ADHD kids who are also autistic may have their autism spotted later, as the ADHD can make it harder to spot some of the autism.
- Bear in mind it's likely that ADHD is underdiagnosed in the UK rather than overdiagnosed.

The world is going to have to change to my child

5

What It's like to Have ADHD

For this book, I have interviewed dozens of people with ADHD: young, old, rich, poor, married or living solo. I asked them how they viewed their brain type – was it a good or bad thing in their life? Only one person said outright that she hated it: she told me she wanted to find every single TikToker gleefully celebrating their ADHD and tell them to fuck off one by one. And only one person said that he loved it – he felt it made him the smartest person in the room. Everyone else had a more nuanced view. Not exactly 'meh' but more 'pros and cons'. One pragmatic man in his twenties told me that whether he likes it or not, he's stuck with it, so he might as well enjoy it.

The person who told me ADHD is brilliant comes across as an alpha-male-type personality. He loves that he always knows where conversations and events are going – it's as if he can fore-see the future. He doesn't take medication but is in the gym from 6.30 to 7.30 a.m. every weekday morning. I assume he's paid a lot of money, not just because the background of our Zoom call in what looks like a very nice home suggests it, but also because he describes walking out of meetings halfway through when he can't cope with listening to people taking ages to get to (or understand) the point. That he can do this and not lose his job is testimony either to an inclusive office culture that is tolerant of difference, or the fact that he makes the company shedloads of money.

What my interviews provided me with was a clear sense that having ADHD is not a barrier to being successful. Among my interviewees were senior doctors, one of whom is well known in her field and often quoted in newspapers. She wanted to remain anonymous for the interview because she said that 'coming out' as ADHD would make it difficult for her as a senior medical professional, as people would assume she makes mistakes. That interview was fascinating: her attention was inconsistent, and although she didn't seem in any way rude or distracted, I didn't get the feeling all her focus was on our discussion. She showed me there is another way to focus, one that allows her inattentive and busy brain to work as it wants to. She may not be 'out', but it was clear she isn't going to exhaust herself by masking – all the stress and energy it would take to pretend she has consistent neurotypical focus is being put to better use building her career.

There were some common themes during these interviews. Not doing great at school despite obviously being clever was a big one. Then there is the 'spiky' profile, which means, for example, that the successful doctor who wins awards for her work can't cook dinner, do the dishes or remember dates with her friends. Alpha Male Man struggles to manage his own money, even though he works at a high level in a financial field.

This gap between appearances and reality can result in shame – and a common theme was: 'If only you knew what was going on inside my brain.' The head teacher whose arms are tattooed, the paramedic who can take control of a life-or-death situation but won't invite anyone to her home because it's too messy. This gap is there with everyone – most of us project an image of how we want to be seen – but with many ADHDers it's bigger and more crafted. It's like carrying a guilty secret all the time, like lugging an invisible rucksack filled with bricks.

Hearing more from people who were enjoying fulfilling careers despite having had difficulties at school made me feel better about the future for M, who is currently out of school. Ditto interviewing people who I found I really liked a lot – like the tattooed head teacher – who told me about their difficulties with friendships when they were young. Perhaps the takeaway message is this: for many of those I spoke to, life got better as they got older. People amass lots of skills after leaving full-time education, and neurodivergent people potentially find it far easier to learn outside school, which is often just a terrible environment for them. Plenty of children who are currently struggling at school and convinced they are thick will end up working as consultants in hospitals, as column writers and financiers.

But I'm falling into the trap of judging success according to a fancy job. On a more meaningful (and less stressful level), I interviewed ADHD people who had settled down and had families and ordinary jobs. They were happy – in the sense that life presented challenges and was up and down, but overall thumbs-up – particularly those who had figured out how to manage their work in a way that didn't give them too much stress and were clear about what they could and couldn't do. Given my sons' battles with anxiety, this is what I really want for them. So sod the impressive-sounding job: if they can just work out how to keep their anxiety within average limits and have friends and loved ones who make them feel clever and loved, that would be the ultimate trophy.

WHAT THE NEUROTYPE IS LIKE . . .
ACCORDING TO ADHD ADULTS

'It's about the match between your environment and your brain'

ADHD has only been a problem at certain parts of my life. It was difficult at school and at university, but when I started work it was fine – only then it became difficult when it was job plus kids. It's about the match between your environment and your brain. Your brain has all these cognitive strengths, as long as the environmental challenges don't get in the way. But of course your environment keeps changing. You keep developing new strategies if you're able to – so life gets better and better – and then, if you're a woman, just as you've figured it all out, you hit menopause and it all goes wrong again.

What I do find difficult is the spiky profile – where you are very good at some things but not at others. This can leave you feeling like a fraud. You know you can perform really high at one level, so why can't you function at another? I can't manage to do the washing-up or make a phone call to a plumber, but I can manage a big meeting with lots of senior doctors. It's also difficult when you enjoy the intellectual stimulation of a big job but the stress of managing it can be challenging. It's about the balance of meeting your potential while looking after your stress levels.

The real challenges are feeling inadequate, feeling like you're underachieving, managing relationships, emotional regulation, mood difficulties, anxiety. It's the patchiness of it – people with ADHD do have good days, when they can do everything, but it isn't consistent, and stress has a big impact on your executive functioning.

When I got diagnosed with ADHD, my psychiatrist asked me how I made it through medical school, and I replied it was because it was all structured and practical – we had to learn about anatomy and pathology, but this wasn't taught in a dry, theoretical way, it was always tied to clinical cases, which kept me interested.

Before medical school, I didn't realise I was clever: I was a C student at school and friendships were very difficult. I was very messy and disorganised and I thought I just had to try harder. I think with ADHD you have to do something you're interested in, work out what works for you and how to make the environment right, and be aware these things take time and you will make loads of mistakes along the way. Failure is part of the process.

Dr Helen Honey, consultant psychiatrist

'I'm constantly telling my brain not to overreact'

I sometimes feel like autism is the serious diagnosis, whereas ADHD has that slight 'everyone has ADHD' vibe to it. Finally you've made sense of why you are this way, then you've got this huge social stigma to overcome.

In the beginning I wanted to tell everyone; now I feel almost embarrassed. It's not that I feel embarrassed about ADHD, it's because it's become trendy and I don't like it. With ADHD you do stupid stuff all the time. You misplace things, you don't read the details. I can get lost in a *straight line. My frustration level is very low, so if someone is boring, I don't have time for it. Small talk irritates me. I used to think I had the worst memory ever – I am a university lecturer and I've got students I taught for three years who I can't remember – but what I've realised is I have a phenomenal memory. I just have to be paying attention for it to work.*

When it comes to trying to handle big emotions, it's hard not to overreact. Often you know you're overreacting but you can't stop. I recently got a shitty email and I was telling my brain, 'Don't do it!', but of course I replied straight away. You try and tell yourself it will pass and hope you don't act, but then the impulsivity kicks in, so you do, then you calm down and think, 'Shit.'

It means I don't trust my emotions a lot of the time. I'm always thinking, 'Is how I feel appropriate?' But also, 'How the hell do I know what is an appropriate emotion?' I'm constantly on my guard.

Kate Lister, newspaper columnist

'I lose everything – including a £20,000 Banksy poster'

I have had to make my peace with losing things because it happens so often. My God, I couldn't even tell you how many expensive umbrellas, handbags, how much make-up I've lost over the years. When I first started to go into town on my own on a shopping trip, every single week without fail I would either lose my wallet or I would do my shopping, get on the bus to come home, get home and be like: 'Where's my shopping?' I often just left it on the bus.

I was that classic away-with-the-fairies girl. That's what everybody would say.

But sometimes it's not a lack of attention, is it? It's sensory overwhelm, overstimulating environments and having a head so full of other things. A million things demanding your attention. If you think about me on a bus trying not to lose my bag, what was really going on is I would have been working hard trying not to forget to get off at my stop, trying not to get lost, trying to remember not to lose my wallet, because I'm always losing my wallet. And so because I'm so busy thinking hard about those things, I suddenly realise I've only got two stops left. Then I panic I'll miss my stop. No wonder I sometimes leave my shopping on the bus with this much going on. It's exhausting.

I used to manage a nightclub in east London and there was a Banksy exhibition there. It was one of his first exhibitions. There was a big piece of work that Angelina Jolie ended up buying for about £1 million. I remember looking at it and thinking, 'My God, it's so amazing.' So I ended up buying a poster for £20. I kept it all rolled up, thinking it would be safest this way. And then one day, after moving house for the fifth time, I thought, 'Oh, where's that Banksy?' And I just had no idea. I looked for it but never found it. The same poster recently sold for £20,000.

Kirsti Hadley, autism and ADHD trainer and speaker

'There is a lot of stigma around ADHD in the black community'

I think I have ADHD and autism but I'm waiting for my assessment. Primary school was okay – I was a high achiever in primary school – only then it all fell apart in secondary where I couldn't focus and had social difficulties. No one ever said to me, 'Is everything okay with you?', or asked me if anything was going on at home, or if I needed adjustments to be made for me to learn and focus better. It was just: 'Get out of my class now. I don't want to speak to you.' There was no compassion: one week I had internal exclusion every single day. It was basically like prison.

I think teachers responded differently to me because I'm black. I didn't feel that way growing up, but now I can see the microaggressions. The school was a predominantly white school and there wasn't anyone I could relate to. As an adult I have worked in a primary school as a head teacher's PA. I can see how children of colour are sometimes treated differently. Take children who throw chairs, kick people and show a lot of anger: the white kids who do this are more likely to get one-on-one teaching assistants and time with teachers, whereas black pupils are more likely to be viewed as being naughty.

Part of this is racism, but part of it is also that some black parents are more likely to see difficulties as a behavioural issue rather than a neurodiverse need. This means they aren't having conversations with the teachers about how it's not about their child being naughty. There is a lot of stigma around ADHD and autism in the black community and a lot of families focus on discipline, which can involve beatings.

There is not enough sitting children down and asking questions to find out what is going on beneath the surface. I was worried when my son was diagnosed: he's a young black boy, he's vulnerable and he's tall for his age, so people assume he's older than he is. So many black kids don't have their needs identified. They are kicked out of school, and some of them then turn to a lifestyle of crime, when in reality no one wants that life. They just need support and to be understood.

Shanelle

'I see ADHD as a massive positive'

There are things I do that others can't. I get things really quickly. Sometimes it's like I'm talking a different language and it takes others ages to catch up so I see ADHD as a massive positive. The fact is you process information rapidly and pivot your discussion before most people have wrapped their heads around the basics. All of that is a real benefit, but there can also be an impact at work. I have been known to stand up to go before meetings have ended, as I get so bored and I'm ready to leave. My boss would sometimes tell me that I had got up before she had finished talking, and I didn't even realise I was doing it. When I was diagnosed I told my boss. She was like, 'Oh really', but then she went home, read up on it and came back and said, 'That literally explains everything.'

It helped as we could then change things. For example my boss used to email me all the time, the moment she thought of something. I couldn't cope. My head has to stay somewhere – I get distracted so easily and she was twisting and turning my attention all the time. We had a chat and she now sends me one email at the beginning or end of the day.

I quite often use music to keep my focus: if I'm reading something that I find difficult, I'll listen to classical, because it doesn't have words, but if I'm writing and it's in my head and needs to come out, I can listen to music with words in. I also have to use music to drown out all the conversation that's happening around me in the office, otherwise I will have a thought on what is being said and join in.

If you spoke to my colleagues they would say I'm excellent with people more junior than me. But I can get totally frustrated with people who are more senior. With them, I'm like, 'Why don't you get it?' My standards are very high. I am high-achieving and I deliver by setting myself targets. If I don't have that direction I could not get things done, so I set myself a goal even if it's an artificial one.

Anonymous man in his forties

'I was told: "You have ADHD." Then the doctor bored me so I stopped listening'

I got diagnosed as autistic at the age of eight, but I wasn't diagnosed with ADHD until I was twenty-six, when I first started working. I noticed that in a nine-to-five job I was expected to be chair-shaped, and in meetings I was like, 'Whoa – why am I finding it so hard to focus?' And my legs couldn't stay still. I would feel like I was going to have an anxiety attack. In some meetings, there was nothing to latch my brain on to, and it was racing, and I thought, 'This isn't autism.'

It felt like instead of spinning inwards, which is what autism feels like at times, ADHD caused me to spin outwards. One day, on my lunch break, I just completely broke down. I went to the occupational health doctor and she was like, 'You have ADHD.' I was like, 'Really? But I have autism.' And she went: 'You can have both.' Then she bored me so I stopped listening.

Getting the ADHD diagnosis was great. It made me feel like, 'Oh, this is why I'm feeling like this, and why I get anxious and why I can't sit still. This is why exercise really helps.' I find the labels help particularly when I'm anxious and when I'm trying to work out whether I need to be: 'What is this to do with? Is it to do with a lack of clarity, or ambiguity, which my autism finds difficult. Or is it to do with my ADHD, the fact that I need to move, and if I don't I will feel like I'm going to explode?'

Camilla Pang, scientist and author

'I wrote the code to the safe on the wall . . . then the shop got broken into'

I was expelled from school when I was fifteen. I didn't get any qualifications, but it didn't matter as I never wanted to go to university, I just wanted to earn money. I got a job at a photo-processing shop in the Bull Ring in Birmingham, was promoted to manager and I had to put the takings in the safe at the end of the day.

It was a nightmare as I could never remember the safe combination. I thought, 'If I write it in a notebook, I'm just going to lose the book.' So I wrote the combination code on the wall above the safe. I didn't think anyone else would see it as it was just me in the shop.

It worked for ages . . . until the shop was broken into and the contents of the safe were stolen. The thieves had read the combination on the wall. I can't remember how much it was but it was pretty much all the day's takings. The police investigated it and there were no CCTV cameras in those days, at least not in the shop, to show I hadn't done it.

The police questioned me and I suddenly realised they suspected me. They never outright said it, but it became clear. They couldn't understand why somebody would write the safe combination code on the wall. And obviously if you're a policeman, you are not going to do this because you understand the risk. But for me, a seventeen-year-old girl with undiagnosed ADHD and autism in a job no one had really taught me how to do, I just thought it was a problem I was solving.

They didn't take it further. I wonder if stereotypes saved me, as they just assumed I was a very ditzy blonde. I was sacked, though, and I assume the owner claimed the amount on insurance, as I didn't hear anything more about it.

Kirsti Hadley, autism and ADHD trainer and speaker

'I keep waiting to fuck up'

I think a lot of my behaviour growing up – which on the surface was extroverted and confident – was really driven by anxiety and stress. It was an act: I ended up masking and putting on a show. I just became louder and louder and embraced this chaotic persona.

The extroverted behaviour became a defence. I leaned into the 'I'll be the funny and loud person' because that made me feel strong and maybe that would help people not care that I couldn't do the serious or important things – or they'd think I was okay with it all. You either feel very shit about yourself or create this persona that gives the impression that you don't care.

I'm still very anxious, which comes from getting things wrong, not quite understanding a situation and not trusting my reactions and processes. I keep waiting to fuck up. If someone sends me an email saying, 'Can we have a chat?', my first thought is: 'I'm going to be fired.'

I like being on my own and I find other people tiring – I burn through my social capital quickly – and that's difficult for people to understand. I really struggle with parties, especially if I am the focus of them. It leaves me drained and overstimulated.

Anonymous man in his thirties

There's one last message to finish with, which I received over the ten months of chats. And that is that ADHD young people need someone who has their back at home. The psychiatrist who made it through the brutal school system of the 1970s and 1980s – whose head teacher, after she spotted her fidgeting in class, drew around her feet with chalk and told her not to step outside – could cope only because her mum told her that her teachers' view of her was rubbish.

While we don't want to create children who are going to make their teachers' and their own lives difficult by being defiant, we need them to know that we are on their side. Always. Whatever problem your child is having, or that the school or your family or outsiders perceive as your child having – well, that's the problem. The problem is never your child.

"Okay brain! We've got a big day today! Please try not to overreact!"

6

To Medicate or Not to Medicate

After we finally got M's ADHD diagnosis, the conversation turned to medication. Did we want to try it? Yes, we did.

M, who was eight at the time, was having a terrible time at school, and, given that the revolution needed for neurodivergent kids in mainstream education is a long way off, the prospect of him taking a pill that could help him listen and focus – and that might just save what scraps of self-esteem he had left – seemed like a no-brainer.

So we walked off with a prescription: 10 mg of Medikinet – a stimulant that is the same as Ritalin, just a different name – to be taken daily. It was okay at first, then the dose was increased too quickly and he hated it. He didn't want to continue with something that made him feel rubbish, so he stopped taking it, and refused to try the lower dose again.

Around this time, his demand avoidance started moving up a few gears in general, and I knew that if I said to him that he should take the pills, then it would never happen. So for six long months I tried my best to pretend I didn't care. I was breezy. I waltzed into the room, plonked down the meds and waltzed out. Take it or don't take it was the vibe. No pressure here! In terms of self-control, this was my Everest. As I made my historic assault on the summit, teeth clamped firmly down on the words that could send me slithering back to base camp, I passed the

stiff bodies of other parents who, unable to hide their desper-
ation, had blurted out: 'Please, take your pills.'

After six months had passed, I made an appointment for him
to see a new psychiatrist. I wasn't convinced about the existing
one (both were private), and within five minutes I knew I had
made the right decision. The new psychiatrist let an anxious M
play *Minecraft* on my phone the whole time during the appointment. He paid attention enough to hear her tell him he was 100
per cent in charge; that medication should not feel horrible but
it was worth trying again, this time with a non-stimulant (atomoxetine). On a piece of paper she listed the possible upsides,
and the downsides. I think she even showed him a graph. He
agreed. Hallelujah!

The following Saturday, he took the pill. No bad side effects
appeared in the morning. *It's going well!!!!!!* I emailed to my
husband, who works on weekends. Then M started to develop
a high temperature, and by the evening he had full-on flu. NOT
EVEN A COLD. He hadn't had flu for years, and it had to pick that
very day to strike. Nothing I could say would convince him that
he was feeling awful not because of the atomoxetine but because
he was unwell.

I was flat out of ideas – and of course, the more he decided
he was done with medication, the more I became convinced it
was the answer to all our problems. Until weeks later, one Sunday evening, staring down the barrel of another awful week at
school, I levelled with him. I was feeling desperate for him to try
the medication as I thought it would make school life a lot easier.
Silence (unusual). Emboldened, I asked: 'What will it take for
you to give it a go?'

Pause. A longer pause (highly unusual). Then came the answer: sixteen sweets.

Deal.

I raced to the corner shop, bought every bag I could grab:
Tangfastics Haribos, normal Haribos, Oreo Bites, strawberry

laces, cola bottles, caramel chocolates in the shape of snakes, Fruittellas, pretty much every single thing ever made by Rowntree's. And in my bedroom, he opened them all and painstakingly, laboriously picked sixteen, as I managed to resist shrieking, FOR THE LOVE OF GOD CAN YOU JUST PICK THEM AND TAKE YOUR PILL. Then he placed them in a pile on my bed, and about a third of the way through unwrapping them and popping each one in his mouth, he took the pill. Oh my God. It had happened.

For the next two weeks, he continued taking his daily pill – but only if he got sixteen sweets a day. Gradually, though, he didn't need to follow the atomoxetine with Haribo chasers. He decided an enormous lollipop would do instead. Then he was content with the smaller Chupa Chups lollipop (why are they so madly difficult to open?). Soon, a mini packet of dried mango did the trick, and then, over time, nothing.

Over those weeks, we started to notice differences at home. M was calmer, less restless and noticeably less demand avoidant. It's hard to know precisely what impact the medication had, as he stopped going to school just after the Sixteen Sweets Sunday, which also reduced his anxiety.

Soon after, at the age of thirteen, my elder son was diagnosed with ADHD (both hyperactive and combined) and started on Medikinet. It made him irritable, so we moved to atomoxetine. That didn't work either, so we're now trying one last medication – guanfacine. He's on 4 mg, and although it makes him miserably knackered, I think he's turning a corner. He's zoning out noticeably less and seems happier, but it is hard to pinpoint if it's the medication causing the increased happiness.

So that's our potted history with medication so far. It's been messy, a work in progress. I worry that it's made my elder son miserable and exhausted, and I'm finding it hard to know if the upside I'm observing is down to the medication.

What has kept me trying is the potential benefits. If you read the research, it's clear that ADHD meds can save lives – they lower the likelihood of the most extreme mental health problems and make it less likely that someone will develop a drink or drug problem, as the reward circuitry of their brain is being sated by pharmaceutical drugs. So in light of this, it's fury-inducing to read newspaper reports of people who view the increase in diagnoses as something other than good news.

But I also genuinely worry that by offering our children pills, we're communicating to them that they aren't acceptable in their unmedicated state. I'm also not sure how my view of neurodiversity squares with giving someone a pill once they've been diagnosed with a neurodivergent condition.

The truth is, your child has to be in charge of the process, because only they know how they feel. If they don't want to take the pills or they are miserable on them – flattened emotionally, or anxious – don't pressure them. The effect of these meds, sometimes in the first few weeks, aren't to be underestimated and can make a person feel massively disoriented, if not sick, before things calm down.

Some adults and older teens hack the medication to fit their lives. They pick and choose. When they need to do a bit of focused work or concentrate and sit still at the theatre, they take their meds. But when they need the creativity that comes with having their brain unfettered and able to function in all its ADHD glory, they don't.

I like this – and plan on continuing the conversation with my two along these lines. The ADHD meds aren't there to make them neurotypical; they are there to help lessen the stress of living in a non-ADHD world.

THE ROLE OF DOPAMINE IN ADHD

My son M loves a doughnut, the jammier the better and, crucially, the sooner the better. He has been known to indulge while we're still in the shop – or rather, to pester until I relent and allow him to indulge.

Doughnuts were how I knew M's ADHD meds were working, and he had more dopamine in his brain. The child who dubs himself the Bottomless Pit wasn't hassling me to eat one right away; in fact I had to ask him if he wanted one. Now frankly astonished, I heard him answer: 'I'll have it when I get home.' He was opting to delay his gratification, and this was significant.

Most ADHD medication boosts levels of dopamine, a neurotransmitting molecule made in your brain that relays messages between your mind and your nerves. You may have heard it described as the 'happy hormone', the 'feel-good hormone' or the 'pleasure molecule', but that is to oversimplify its role. The dopamine system is designed, from an evolutionary standpoint, to reward you when you're doing the things you need to do to survive – eat, drink, run away at speed from the tiger and reproduce, not necessarily in that order.

In his book *Behave: The Biology of Humans at Our Best and Worst*, the eminent American neuroscientist Robert Sapolsky observes that having sex releases dopamine in every species that scientists have taken the time to observe in the throes of passion. For most humans, just thinking about sex is enough to trigger a rush of dopamine, and men get a greater dose than women when they view sexually arousing visual stimuli. Chronic stress or pain depletes dopamine. Drugs such as cocaine, heroin and alcohol create a tsunami.

But dopamine's role is more complicated than just doing the basics to keep us alive (and procreating). It is there to guide us to make the more responsible choice. Sapolsky tells of a study that monitored the dopamine levels of two people playing the filthy capitalist's board game of choice, Monopoly. Two scenarios were tested out: the first where the players cooperated and both received a moderate reward; and the second where one stabbed the other in the back and got a bigger reward. The result? 'While

93

both outcomes increased [dopamine] activity, the bigger increase occurred after cooperation.'

The interesting thing about dopamine is this, though: once you know you will get a reward from an activity – let's say, completely at random, that first sip of wine once the kids are in bed – the amount of dopamine released by that swig decreases, and the amount you get *anticipating* it increases. In another trial, monkeys in a darkened room were given a raisin after the light was turned on. Over time, their levels of dopamine began to decrease when they got the raisin and to increase when the light went on. Dopamine is our brain's way of encouraging us to wait for our raisins, and to not give up.

Together with other functions in the brain, it is there to guide us to do the harder, more correct thing with the benefit not being felt immediately – to pass the famous psychological test of the 1970s in which children could choose to have one marshmallow now or two if they waited. Being able to make the right long-term decision is the bedrock of executive function, the skill set that allows us to plan and organise.

Sapolsky adds that humans are unique in our ability to delay gratification for long periods of time – or as he puts it: 'No warthog restricts calories to look good in a bathing suit next summer.' But in people with ADHD, he concludes, there are 'abnormalities in dopamine response profiles during temporal discounting tasks' – those that require delayed gratification.

It has been suggested that ADHDers may have low levels of dopamine because they are high in dopamine transporters, a protein that acts a bit like a toilet flush, carrying the neurotransmitter away. Too many transporters means too much transporting, which means the dopamine can disappear down the pan before it has done its job.

One way ADHD medication increases the levels of dopamine is by blocking these transporters. If you have too many dopamine transporters delivering, then there is less help connecting neurons in the brain so they talk to one another. This can make it harder to sit still and focus on boring tasks.

Dopamine also helps control things like attention, sleep, arousal, mood and movement, as well as encouraging us to try things again if we don't succeed immediately. Dopamine levels can be affected by stress: if someone is highly stressed, such as a pupil experiencing sensory overload in a classroom or struggling to sit still and concentrate, their levels will fall.

If you have a regulated dopamine system, you are likely to feel happy, motivated, alert and focused for a reasonable amount of your day. Too little dopamine, and you can feel tired and unmotivated and struggle to concentrate.

As humans, our brains are hard-wired to seek out behaviours that release dopamine in our reward system, and an unmedicated ADHDer may be left trying to constantly improve their dopamine levels by taking drugs, drinking too much alcohol, eating sugary food, having lots of sex, creating a scene, getting into trouble or stressful situations, hitting the gym once/twice a day, listening to music on headphones. High-risk activities – driving fast, sky diving – are also very effective ways to elicit a dopamine spike.

ADHD people are overrepresented in jobs that come with urgency or deadlines: paramedics, live TV, emergency doctors and news desks. The deadline and stress provides the dopamine that allows them to focus. They wouldn't be able to do this if the deadline was a month away or there wasn't any urgency.

HOW DO ADHD DRUGS WORK?

Stimulants

Stimulants work by increasing levels of the neurotransmitters dopamine and norepinephrine in the brain.

Dopamine, as we know, plays a major role in executive function, the set of skills and brain processes you need to get stuff done, while norepinephrine is important for paying attention and feeling alert.

Methylphenidate – Medikinet, Concerta, Equasym are different brand names for this drug, as is Ritalin in the US – is what is known as the 'first line' medication for ADHD – i.e. the first one a doctor will prescribe, unless there is a reason not to. This is because it works quickest and well for the vast majority. Research shows it has a positive impact for between 70 and 80 per cent of people who try it.

There are different types of stimulants, which do the same thing but over different timescales. Which one is best for your child depends on their biochemistry and what other conditions, if any, they have.

Stimulants are controlled drugs, as there is potential for abuse (i.e. getting addicted to it if not taken as prescribed). This means you may have to prove your identity when collecting your prescription. You have to pick it up within twenty-eight days and you can only get one month's lot of pills in one go. Any teens or young adults with a history of drug problems are likely to be prescribed non-stimulants.

It is likely that stimulants will affect your child's sleep, and appetite will be reduced while on them. Often children who take them in the morning eat a large breakfast and dinner but not lunch, and they may not be prescribed to children who can't afford to lose weight.

In terms of impact on sleep, melatonin is typically offered to help counter this. Melatonin is a hormone, not a drug, and is replacing some of what is naturally produced to help us nod off – something that neurotypical people have in spades but for some annoying reason neurodivergent people don't (or at least not at the right time). Melatonin has made an enormous difference for both my boys and I'm an evangelist for its use.

Another thing to consider is that stimulants only work for a certain time period before they wear off (while non-stimulants are effective around the clock). 'Rebound' is the term for when you have an agitated and tearful child who is feeling the effect of the stimulants wearing off. It tends to have a bigger impact when they are on an immediate-release form of stimulant, rather than a slow-release form, which can cause less rebound. (Non-stimulants tend not to have a rebound in this way.)

Dr Helen Honey, consultant psychiatrist at CAMHS for deaf children, who is ADHD herself, says: 'Rebound is much more common in some medications – some of the medications come off more gradually, others drop off more suddenly. People talk about the "Concerta Crash", and generally it lasts thirty minutes. You can feel grumpy, tired, demotivated and tearful. It does seem to get better when you have been on the medication longer. Rebound time is when I recommend screen time for kids or intense exercise. And you can imagine which of the two options is more likely.'

Of her patients who do get on with drugs, she says they describe being able to concentrate better, they get into less trouble at school, there is less chatter in their brain. 'It becomes easier to do hard things,' she says. 'I have had kids who take medication who were having huge problems and have since massively thrived. The evidence is that you should pursue environmental support – as in changing the environment – as well as medication. I worry that if schools and parents go straight to medication and feel they don't have to change anything else, well, that's not fair. I normally say to kids: "This is a team effort – we can't just do medication."'

What are the different stimulant meds and what do they do?

The most common stimulant is **methylphenidate**. Brand names include Medikinet and Tranquilin. All are short-acting, with effects that last four hours. This means they get to work fast and wear off rapidly and are often taken multiple times a day – usually morning, lunchtime and afternoon. Longer-acting types, effective for up to twelve hours, include Concerta XL, Medikinet XL and Equasym XL. The long-acting stimulants are generally taken once in the morning and that's it, which means your child does not have to take tablets again during school hours.

Possible side effects: increase in blood pressure and heart rate; loss of appetite; trouble sleeping (often people are prescribed melatonin to counteract this); headaches; stomach aches; feeling aggressive, depressed, anxious or tense; can also affect growth.

Another common stimulant is **lisdexamfetamine** (brand name Elvanse, among others), which is prolonged release and lasts up to fourteen hours. This is usually offered to people when methylphenidate hasn't worked.

Possible side effects: loss of appetite and weight loss; aggression; sleepiness; dizziness; headaches; diarrhoea; nausea and vomiting.

Non-stimulants

For 20–30 per cent of people with ADHD, stimulants don't work. It may be that these drugs make them too anxious or angry, or they are thin and don't have any more weight to lose. For them, non-stimulants are usually the next option a psychiatrist considers.

Non-stimulants tend to focus more on increasing levels of norepinephrine, which helps with alertness, attention and focus, with some raising levels of serotonin, also known as the 'happy hormone'. Views and research on their efficacy vary: some trials show them not to be as effective for the same proportion of people as stimulants; others show they are as effective but take a lot longer – over six months – to reach that point, as they work better as time goes on.

There are usually fewer problems with sleep, and parents in research studies say there is less of the 'emotional blunting' that can be reported with stimulants. Non-stimulants don't become effective immediately, as stimulants do, and it can take several months before you see the full impact. And if your child misses taking a pill, it may affect their blood pressure (which needs to be checked regularly, at least in the initial stages of prescribing). This may not be an issue at lower doses, but in higher doses a child may feel dizzy. One upside is that the drugs work twenty-four hours a day, so there's no rebound.

'There isn't really the on/off with the non-stimulants as there is with the stimulants,' says Dr Honey. 'It can be good for autistic kids with ADHD – they prefer a steady state of being.'

What are the different non-stimulant meds and what do they do?

Atomoxetine

While stimulants tend to increase dopamine, atomoxetine is what is known as a 'selective norepinephrine reuptake inhibitor', which means it works by increasing levels of norepinephrine. It does this by stopping the transporter

---

cells from getting rid of the norepinephrine before its job has been done.

Atomoxetine was initially developed as an antidepressant – something it wasn't very good at. But then it was noticed that people with ADHD did well on it. It works gradually, and after three months about 50 per cent of people who take it find it helpful. By six months, the figure is 70 per cent.

Some studies show that atomoxetine is better than stimulants at helping anxiety, and some practitioners find it beneficial for people who are both ADHD and autistic. For my demand avoidant son, it resulted in a decrease in some of his anxiety around demands.

There are concerns around suicide ideation as a very rare side effect, although the merits of this concern have been debated over the years. In the US, there used to be a 'black box' warning – the strongest warning – on the box, which led to clinicians prescribing it less. The warning came after a study carried out in 2005 involving 1,357 young people and adolescents appeared to show a significantly higher risk of suicidal thoughts in patients taking it compared with those who took stimulants. Five reported suicide ideation and there was one attempt, all taking place in children younger than twelve within thirty-two days of treatment.

But in 2016, another piece of research was done and found a different result: that there was no difference in the rate of suicide ideation for young people on atomoxetine compared with taking stimulants. The study was vast, involving half a million children between the ages of five and eighteen over a four-year period. Now atomoxetine is being prescribed in bigger numbers, and Dr Russell Barkley, the well-known US-based neuropsychiatrist, believes the black-box warning was an 'absurd' overreaction to the data. He points out that the risk of suicide ideation among young people not taking atomoxetine is far greater than among those who take it (6 per cent compared with 0.37 per cent).

Possible side effects: loss of appetite; effect on height (though this is less likely than with stimulants); increase in blood pressure and heart rate; nausea and vomiting; stomach aches; trouble sleeping; dizziness, irritability and headaches. More serious and rarer side effects include liver damage.

Guanfacine (brand name Intuniv)

Guanfacine is in a class of medications known as alpha-2 agonists. First developed to treat high blood pressure, these drugs relax blood vessels, reducing blood pressure in the process. But scientists believe they also target an area of the brain that regulates attention and impulsivity, which is why they are prescribed to ADHDers, and reduce the emotional responses of the amygdala – the part of the brain that controls these things. Dr William Dodson, the psychiatrist who featured in an earlier chapter of this book – the man who coined the term 'rejection sensitive dysphoria' and who could see this was a central feature for ADHDers – has said he has found guanfacine to be particularly helpful for his patients coping with RSD. It is available in liquid form if your child can't take tablets, and can also help with physical tics.

My elder son is on this drug and I think it's helping; as I said earlier, I'm particularly noticing a reduction in zoning out. I can't go into specifics as he's a mortified teen, but I'm happy, although he is often very tired, which can get him down so it's definitely a trade-off. For most, the sleepiness doesn't last beyond one to two weeks, but for E it hasn't fully gone away – particularly when he wakes – though adjusting the time we give him the medication (and giving it to him twice a day, rather than in one dose) has helped.

Clonidine (brand name Catapres or Kapvay)

Clonidine works similarly to guanfacine and is good for young people who are anxious. It can also help with sleep, and some sleep clinics add it to sleep medication in very low doses. Both drugs can both be used in conjunction with stimulants, which typically help more with focus.

Possible side effects of guanfacine and clonidine: extreme tiredness (which can be temporary); feeling weak; dry mouth; headache; irritability; stomach pain, nausea and constipation.

HOW DO PSYCHIATRISTS WORK OUT THE BEST MEDICATION?

Experience and patience. They will have observed how different drugs have worked with different patients and spotted patterns: which ones work for certain issues and personalities, for example. Sometimes clinicians will opt for both stimulants and non-stimulants to get the best treatment.

Working out which is the right medication is a process of supervised trial and error. Even family members may experience different results with the same medication, so it can be a hard process to predict. The optimal dose varies between individuals. It may need to be titrated – changed regularly – in the early days, and monitoring for side effects is also needed in order to establish the best dose. A 'start low, go slow' approach, where the drug can be gradually increased, is usually best. We didn't do this with my younger son and I regretted it. If your child feels very irritable or anxious or seems flatter emotionally after, say, two weeks, you need to raise this with the prescribing doctor, as it isn't fair to keep a child feeling this way for longer than necessary.

WHAT IT'S LIKE TO TAKE MEDICATION WHEN YOU HAVE ADHD?

I asked ADHDers about their experience and view of medication. Below are some of the responses – which range from 'changed my life' to 'I like my brain as it is and don't want to change it, thank you very much'. One poster on Reddit described the feeling of being still as 'almost overwhelming . . . I imagine neurotypicals take that stillness for granted'.

> *I get told off less at school and feel more shy.*
> **One eight-year-old about how she feels when taking Elvanse**

> *I tried three different types of ADHD meds and they made me feel really anxious. It doesn't happen to everyone but ADHD meds can make you feel worse. I think it can be a difficult message that family and friends prefer a person medicated. You can be left feeling like you are constantly annoying and have to change yourself.*
> **Kirstie McStay, community manager at Spectrum Gaming**

It makes me feel more calm.

A fourteen-year-old boy who takes Medikinet

I had no idea how noisy my brain was until I took it. Thousands of thoughts all at the same time, competing, sensory overload and suddenly it's silent. OH MY GOD. After starting medication, I realised how filthy my flat was and time seemed to last for ever. I'd be constantly looking at the clock and it was only 10 a.m. I realised how much of my time I used to spend daydreaming. I would talk to people I'd known for years and think: 'Have you always been this boring?' I spoke to a nurse about suddenly finding my friends boring and she said, 'It's because you're actually listening to them now.' Before the drugs I felt like I wasn't fully engaging with the world around me.

When your brain is vivid, colourful and chaotic, pre-medication, you're used to that. Then suddenly, when you are on the medication, you focus on one thing and it can be very disorientating. It took me five to six months to get used to it. It's like when you have bad eyesight and you try glasses for the first time and you're like, 'Oh my God, is that what the world looks like to everyone else?'

Kate Lister, newspaper columnist

I take Elvanse. The medication has been life-changing, because I can be sure about my energy levels every day and life feels a bit more consistent. It doesn't take away all of the forgetfulness or the rejection sensitivity but it leaves you on a much more even keel, more able to regulate your emotions. I still go up and down with my emotions but it's nowhere near how I was before.

Kirsti Hadley, autism and ADHD speaker and trainer

When I started the assessment process for ADHD, I wanted to try medication because I was getting frustrated. Two years later I'm not sure I still want to. Most of the things I wanted medication for were things based on other people's standards: writing boring reports, being able to regularly tidy the house. It's okay to not be able to do those things. Also when I'm really passionate I can come up with twelve ideas, and get pure joy out of all the ideas, and medication might stop that. When you have medication the things that are hard become easier but then the things that are more exciting become less exciting. It can make you flatter.

I know some people do find medication really helpful, but it's horrific that young people get this message that they can't be who they are, and I don't feel comfortable passing that on. I know some people who are just on their medication for school hours, or a friend who just does it nine to five while at work and then he's free.

Andy Smith, Spectrum Gaming

NON-MEDICATION OPTIONS THAT HAVE A SIMILAR EFFECT

Fish oils

Researchers from King's College London and China Medical University in Taichung, Taiwan, have found that omega-3 fish oil supplements improve attention among children with ADHD, but only for those with low levels of omega-3 in their blood. Some doctors will recommend this, particularly for families who don't want to try medication, as the benefit of fish oil was found in one study to be close to the benefit of medication for those with low levels. The study wasn't huge (involving ninety-two young people), and was carried out in Taiwan, where diets usually contain more oily fish compared to the UK. Previously studies have showed more conflicting results, so more research needs to be done before we know for sure the role of omega-3. It is also a good idea to make sure your children get enough vitamin D, as this is involved in the production of dopamine and norepinephrine. Most of us don't get enough of this vitamin.

Exercise

Exercise releases dopamine, norepinephrine and serotonin – the same hormones boosted by ADHD medication. This means that after exercise, ADHD people are often better able to focus and carry out tasks requiring executive function skills – research has shown that in particular, working memory and cognitive flexibility (the ability to easily switch between tasks) improves. In addition to this, exercise affects how our amygdala (the part of the brain that reacts to real or imagined threats) interprets information. The amygdala can blunt the hair-trigger responses, so we may be less likely to scream at a friend or parent in a fit of rage when things don't go our way. As a friend once said to me: on the days he goes for a run, he feels like the world isn't out to get him in the way he feels it is on the days he doesn't go.

An analysis of twenty-three studies looking at the impact of exercise on ADHD, published in *Frontiers*, a magazine for psychiatrists, shows that exercise helps across the board, but it particularly helps people with inattentive ADHD. The research also points to some studies suggesting that the impact on young people's brains is greater compared with adults. However, a note of caution is sounded, pointing out a lack of rigour in some of the studies. At the moment there is no evidence to suggest exercise is an effective alternative therapy to medication, or exactly what type of exercise helps best and how long the effects last. Most professionals, with the information they have so far, recommend exercise in addition to medication. This is not to deny that some adults, particularly those in the gym every day, have found that exercise is a very effective alternative to medication; just that this hasn't been proven to be true. Part of this is down to the fact that while non-stimulant medication lasts twenty-four hours and stimulants lasts up to fourteen hours, it's not clear how long the spike in dopamine and norepinephrine lasts after an exercise session. Anecdotal evidence suggests an hour, or maybe ninety minutes, of calm and clarity. For this reason some doctors recommend exercise in the morning if possible, and taking medication about an hour later, when the immediate focusing effects of exercise begin to wear off.

Some studies suggest that exercises requiring more thought (martial arts, gymnastics) may end up with better results than just running on a treadmill. This may be because the different individual skills required – including balance and hand–eye coordination – have a positive impact on a larger number of parts of the brain compared with the treadmill.

It needs to be said that exercise isn't always easy for neurodivergent folk, who are often (like my two) also dyspraxic. In

107

addition, the idea of ADHD people having endless energy to run Duracell Bunny style can be a myth: for ADHDers the reality is that energy cycles can feel very boom and bust, with knackered-ness a real issue. But obviously there is no downside to regular exercise and there are many reasons why your ADHD child should do it – it only makes everything better in the long term, as I tell my elder son when I nag him to come with me to the gym. Here we do weights and boxing with the ever-patient Omer, our personal trainer, who does a thirty-minute session with both of us. While I really want to be lazy and scroll my phone as my son works on his core, it is one of those times when I have to lead by example. And so for the sake of introducing good habits, this lazy middle-aged mum who can't ride a bike and whose favourite hobby is watching true-crime documentaries now hits the gym first thing every Sunday. The six-pack is nowhere near in sight, but my right hook is improving weekly. Bam.

TL;DR

A summary of the chapter. It was rather long, after all – here's a shortcut.

- ADHD drugs work by increasing levels of the neurotransmitters dopamine and norepinephrine in the brain.
- Dopamine plays a major role in executive function, the set of skills and brain processes you need to get stuff done, while norepinephrine is important for paying attention and feeling alert.
- Stimulants only work for a certain time period before they wear off (while non-stimulants are effective around the clock). 'Rebound' is the term for what happens when you want to burst into tears or scream the house down when they wear off. (Good time for screens or exercise.)

- Non-stimulants tend to focus more on increasing levels of norepinephrine, which also helps with alertness, attention and focus, with some raising levels of serotonin (also known as the 'happy hormone'). They take longer to become effective.
- ADHDers who take medication talk about the relief of being able to focus consistently; others talk about medication causing horrible anxiety and emotional blunting.
- Exercise boosts levels of the same neurotransmitters that ADHD drugs do and some adults use it as an alternative, though it is thought the benefits wear off more quickly than they do with medication.
- Some ADHD adults 'hack' their medication – they take it when they have a work task that requires consistent focus or if they are going to the theatre, but not at other times when they want the unfettered creativity their brain brings.

7

Executive Dysfunction

ADHD people are natural interrupters. But while disruption is a prized ability in the business world, when it happens conversationally too many times, it gets annoying.

I am a natural interrupter, and grew up in a family where this was the norm. The first half of my life I was oblivious to the fact that it was a problem, but even when I did twig, it was difficult to remedy. I was once in a newspaper conference, a meeting where all the senior editors have a formal discussion about the day's stories, and I interrupted the editor as he was making a point. Every head in the room swivelled in my direction and I garbled an apology, feeling a red-hot wave of shame wash over me for being conversationally rubbish once again.

My younger son is like me. Trying to drill social niceties into him we used to tell him to wait for a gap in the conversation before he took control of proceedings. 'Was there a gap?' we would hector him after yet another instance of conversational hijacking. As soon as there was a microsecond's pause in a chat he would shout 'GAP!' and spill into that imperceptible slice of dead air with what he wanted to say. And of course, when I interrupted him, he'd roar: 'MUM! WAS THERE A GAP?!'

But is interrupting such a great moral failing? Sure, it's not good to interrupt your boss or anyone else at work because it means meetings become chaotic – and long. But as with so many (neurotypical) social skills, if something doesn't come to you easily, you are framed as being a thoughtless, bad person. You interrupt, therefore you don't care what other people are saying and you are just lacking self-control. This is way too harsh, however, as there is no attempt to understand what causes someone to interrupt.

One reason ADHDers are more prone to interrupting is down to executive function difficulties. Executive function is the very wide-ranging set of mental skills that help you to start a task, sequence it and not get distracted from it; to resist acting impulsively and see it through. One of the skills involved in this is working memory – holding a thought in your head – which is something ADHDers find difficult, hence the need to get the thought out there before it drops out of your brain. Combine this with impulsivity and you get that tendency to interrupt.

Another working theory I have is that ADHDers with their quick-acting brains often just get the point of the conversation quicker, then have to wait ages for the neurotypicals in the room to catch up – which is even more punishing when you have a low boredom threshold. I tweeted this theory on X, and the responses I received were fascinating – as you will read below.

Child or adult, you should not interrupt to your heart's content, and the other person should be allowed to get a word in edgeways. To expect others to endlessly listen to you and have no points of their own to make is not reasonable. But we need to have more understanding and empathy for executive function difficulties. Nobody would dream of punishing a kid who is a wheelchair user for not being able to walk, but for some reason it's fine to give ADHD kids detentions for forgetting things, poor organisation, or other issues related around their executive functioning.

So, if your child is super chatty and interrupty, take time to notice what it takes for them not to do these things more. If you are a teacher, appreciate the effort it takes for an ADHD student not to shout out their amazing point to the whole class, even though their body is screaming at them to do it.

The traditional answer to some of these difficulties has been to pack your kid off to a social skills class so they can learn to make friends like a neurotypical (and likely hate themselves more when they fail). But this isn't the way forward. Neurotypicals need to develop more understanding – and become less judgemental – and sometimes allow conversations to happen according to other people's rules.

While we wait for understanding of executive function and social differences to develop, tell your child you know how hard it is for them to listen and not interrupt. Guide them to learn listening skills and strategies, which can be improved and extended with practice, making life easier not only for the people around them, but for your child too. At the same time explain that when they find themselves interrupting, it does not make them a bad person. Explain what neurotypical social skills and rules are, and how neurotypicals can get frustrated when those rules aren't observed. Some neurotypical social skills have value, but not all – and ADHD and autistic people have some very underappreciated social skills too. Convey that there isn't a 'right' way to socialise or be a friend, but it can make life easier to be aware of what the neuro-majority expects at school or at work.

Below are the enlightening answers to my interrupting theory from people on X – which range from 'I am not aware I'm doing it' to 'the thoughts will fall out of my head if I don't.'

I'm convinced I 'hear' the end of the other person's sentence in my head and start answering, then realise too late they haven't actually finished talking.

I interrupt my partner constantly, and it drives her up the wall. I don't even realise I'm doing it sometimes, for me it's a case of 'Oh I'll help by giving the response ASAP.'

I have ADHD but I'm also Jewish, which means in my extended family cooperative overlapping is the norm, so people get interrupted all the time and that's just how conversation works. I can't tell to what extent my interrupting is ADHD vs being Jewish.

I do it because I'm scared about forgetting what I'm going to say . . . also over-empathising and keen to make the connection.

I get an idea and it will fly out of my head if I don't explain it immediately. I have to write it down to stop myself blurting it out. Also while I'm trying to retain the idea in my head, I'm unable to focus on anything that is being said around me.

People talk for five full minutes, but maybe thirty seconds of that included everything that was needed, and I often find myself tuning out while I wait for the unnecessary sentences to end.

WHAT ARE EXECUTIVE FUNCTION SKILLS?

Executive functions are basically the 'getting shit done skills' – or to put it more academically, the set of mental skills you need to execute a task. These skills are the processes your brain uses to get organised, plan something, initiate work, stay on task, regulate your emotions, ignore the impulses telling you to leap out from behind your desk and run into the playground, be adaptable and resilient. They are often compared to the air-traffic control system at a busy airport: just as it manages the arrivals and departures of different aircraft on different runways, so the brain uses these skills to filter distractions, prioritise tasks, set and achieve goals.

Good executive function skills make school – and life – far easier. A child with executive function (EF) difficulties, meanwhile, will find it hard to manage to bring their maths book in on the right day, to do their homework, to remember when they have to hand it in and to show their parents the note from school festering at the bottom of the bag along with the empty crisp packet and the blackened banana skin. Getting them to tidy their room is like starting World War III. They lose their coat or leave it at school regularly. You have to hover like a hawk to get them to do their maths. You start to wonder if there will ever be a time when you don't have to stage-manage your child's life.

ADHD is often framed as an executive function disorder. While difficulties in this area are very common among neurodivergent people in general, they peak with ADHDers. I remember going to my son's specialist school for the first time and nearly laughing out loud when I saw they had an entire lost property room rather than the solitary basket his mainstream primary used.

Academic research has found that children with ADHD are about two to three years behind their neurotypical peers in the development of certain areas of their brain, such as the prefrontal cortex, responsible for executive functioning. Meanwhile, adults with ADHD are thought to develop only 75–80 per cent of their executive functioning capacity compared with their non-ADHD peers. Stress can reduce executive functioning too, so I would unscientifically suggest we can easily knock off a few more percentage points for that, given how much neurodivergent people have to be stressed about.

So central to school life and learning are EF skills that some scientists believe they have more influence on grades than a person's IQ. This will come as no surprise to any parent who sees their clearly very clever neurodivergent child merely scrape by, or fail, at school.

We will come on to exactly what these skills entail, but first an idea of what is known as 'executive dysfunction', which is what life is like when you have difficulties in this area. And because executive functions involve so many processes inside your brain, executive dysfunction can take a number of forms. Some examples:

- Difficulty motivating yourself to start a task, particularly one that seems difficult or uninteresting.
- Difficulty planning a task.
- Struggling to move from one task to another.
- Getting distracted part way through a task, causing you to misplace items or lose your train of thought (like leaving your keys in the refrigerator because you wanted a snack, but your hands were full so you put your keys down inside the fridge and forgot about them).
- Struggling with thinking before you talk, causing you to blurt out the first thing that pops into your head without considering that it might hurt someone's feelings.
- Having trouble explaining your thought process clearly, because you understand it in your head but you aren't very good at ordering it in a logical way for the listener.

How executive dysfunction feels

Shitty is the short answer. Women have described executive dysfunction as like going through the brain fog and symptoms of the menopause every day. Shudder. Ordinary tasks can reduce a person to tears, or get constantly postponed or not done. It's inertia for the things that are remotely difficult, a barrier between you and the task. It feels heavy, and can leave people with feelings of intense shame. Why can't they complete tasks easily that others can? What's wrong with them?

I saw a post on X that I thought powerfully summed it up. It said that ADHD is 'spending all day trying not to interrupt people, having to start the same task over and over because you lost focus – literally having to summon the power of Thor just to transition from one task to another . . . and then wondering why you're so tired.'

What makes it worse is the fact that, because awareness of executive dysfunction is so low, children are not told there is a good reason why they find these so-called simple tasks difficult; that it's not just them being lazy or stupid. Difficulty with EF is why adult ADHDers can find it impossible to fill in forms, not to mention doing the washing-up, budgeting, making dinner, doing housework. People in this situation describe feeling like they are 'shit at life' or failing at adulting.

As I mentioned earlier, EF skills are controlled, for the most part, by the prefrontal cortex of the brain, the area that regulates decision-making and plans and organises for the future, and the place where ADHD brains have 'weaker function', in the words of the medical researchers. It is thought this part of the brain matures later for people with ADHD, and parts of the prefrontal cortex have been found to be smaller according to some studies (while other parts of the ADHD brain are larger).

In his book *Behave*, Robert Sapolsky explains how tasks that increase the cognitive load on the prefrontal cortex – taking

117

a tough working-memory test, regulating social behaviour or making numerous decisions about shopping – leave people less 'prosocial' afterwards: less charitable or helpful, more likely to lie. Basically, they put you in a bad mood. So anyone with problems with EF and a prefrontal cortex that isn't running as smoothly and efficiently as it might is going to be in a bad mood a lot of the time.

Can you fix executive dysfunction?

Everything about school is a test of our EF skills: the expectation that you wait your turn in class, put your hand up before speaking, submit your homework on time, start learning when your teacher wants you to, don't get distracted, pack your bag before and after lessons, remember to bring your PE kit on the right day, cope with an exam . . . all these things require high-level EF skills, which ADHD kids typically do not have.

It's important to note that not everyone is convinced there is a need to roar into action, and that potentially the EF differences experienced by ADHD people need to be accommodated and understood rather than fixed. Marta Rose, an American woman who created and directs Divergent Design Studios, an online community for neurodivergent creatives, has an interesting take. She has written about how successful men have historically outsourced their executive functioning to women, such as their wives and secretaries – 'someone to keep the house, raise the kids, keep track of the calendar, plan, shop and execute the relentless daily tasks'.

She has proposed an alternative model to the executive function value system: design thinking. 'To actually get things done,' she writes, we should expect 'both periods of high-energy and fast-paced productivity as well as times that are dreamy, restful and obsessively inefficient'.

As ever, there is a compromise: have a conversation with your child about how executive function skills make life easier in a neurotypical world, and explain that it's worth trying to improve some areas around this, but be clear that the goal isn't to have the executive function skills of a neurotypical, as that is a hiding to nothing. The goal is to have the EF skills of a neurodivergent person who can cope with school and life.

People – and by people, I mean neurotypicals – can be very unforgiving of poor organisational skills, and see them as a personal failing. A few years ago, my husband and I sold our flat to a couple who were enraged that some of our post continued to arrive through their door. We had arranged for it to be automatically redirected for six months, but after that point there were still stragglers arriving. The husband made it clear he found this unacceptable, and appeared frustrated by my inability to remember every single organisation I had ever given my details to so I could ask them to update their mailing lists. I ended an exchange on WhatsApp by being very rude – then like a coward blocked his number so I couldn't read the reply. I felt triumphant: take that, intolerant person! That feeling is still mostly intact a year later, though it can falter when I see one of them, which happens more often than I'd like since we only moved around the corner, and every time we must go through the awkward pretence of not having seen each other. But still: worth it.

You can never train yourself out of being a forgetful person, so it's important for neurodivergent people to cut themselves some slack and come up with strategies and workarounds: if it's swimming on a Tuesday, encourage your child to leave the bag with their swimming stuff by the door, so they trip over it when leaving the house. Stick a whiteboard somewhere obvious and write your weekly schedule on it, so everyone is less likely to forget it's swimming day.

THINGS YOUR CHILD IS LIKELY TO NEED SUPPORT WITH

Below is a summary of some of the areas that executive function skills affect, just to give you an idea of how wide and varied these skills are – and what the impact is when they are not there.

Planning and prioritising can be tricky, and a child may need help working out what the aim or goal of the task is. They may also find it hard to work out what steps will help achieve that goal. Breaking the task down into steps will help.

Your child may also have difficulties with **working memory**. This is a form of memory that allows a person to temporarily hold a limited amount of information at the front of their mind for immediate use; for ADHDers, this information may drop out of the mind too soon. This can make following instructions hard, particularly if there are lots of different steps, while waiting your turn to speak is also a challenge (you fear you will forget the point you want to make).

Organisation is almost certain to be problematic thanks to difficulties in these areas, which could involve struggling to make decisions (including decision paralysis), losing things, being unable to balance multiple tasks, needing to write appointments down in your diary immediately (if not, they're forgotten). This is not to say that all ADHDers are terrible with organisation – some become brilliant at it, as a way of overcompensating – just that it's not as easy as it is for someone who doesn't have EF difficulties, and some people will never be great at it, no matter how hard they try.

Task initiation – the ability to start a task without faffing about can be hard. As can flexible thinking: adapting or responding to change by revising thoughts or plans.

The route to a stress-free morning (okay . . . less stressful)

I'm taking a wild guess here. You have not been blessed with a child who finds it easy to get ready for school. Your child does not naturally wake up and cheerfully get dressed unaided, pop their bread in the toaster, brush their teeth without fuss, and they have not packed their bag the night before, remembering which books and sports kit to bring. You may instead have a family like mine, which involves two adults with their own difficulties managing their stress levels as they try to herd two recalcitrant kids on a massive go-slow who aren't exactly jumping for joy at the prospect of going to school and who have all the above EF difficulties. The result is like trying to push a massive boulder up a hill every morning, while attempting – and failing – to stay calm, because if you get stressed, you lose your grip on the boulder and it rolls back down the hill, flattening you along the way. Then you have to peel yourself off the floor and try not to cry because you are back to square one, having to start the whole exhausting process again. I am not ashamed to admit that trying to get my two to school – or one, as it's been lately – can leave me close to tears.

Peg Dawson, the queen of executive function strategies, in her book *Smart but Scattered*, recommends taking the checklist below and doing a dry run the night before. Your child could pretend to be in bed asleep (if they aren't a teen; if they are, this request could cause the most extreme of eye rolls), and you walk in and say, 'Rise and shine!' They then pretend to get dressed, ticking the 'done' column, before going downstairs and pretending to eat breakfast, and so on. Then when they use the list for real, you can prompt them through the steps, until the process becomes automatic, at which point you can fade into the background. I don't know exactly how long things can take to become automatic, but I have been told it can be several months. 'Mistakes are often made in failing to provide adequate support long enough for the child to acquire the skill and in failing to reduce the supports gradually,' writes Dawson.

Getting ready for school checklist

Task	Done?
Wake up	
Get dressed	
Eat breakfast	
Take ADHD meds	
Clean teeth	
Wash face	
Pack school bag	
Feed fish	

Praising kids is important too: 'I like the way you got dressed with only one reminder from me'; 'Thank you for showing self-control when your brother teased you'; 'I was impressed you were able to stop playing on your iPad without absolutely losing your shit when it was time to come down for dinner' (or words to that effect).

The key thing I've learnt about EF skills is that you mustn't do them for your child, which in retrospect is what I've definitely being doing for too long. The child ideally needs to develop the skills to do these things for themselves, and if they at least part-design the schedule, they are going to be much more motivated to stick to it.

That means planning things together. If your child has an exam coming up, don't roar into action and compile the revision time-table yourself; instead, ask what their strategy is for preparing for the exam. Sow the seed, then, when it's (hopefully) germinated, work out together what their timetable looks like. It's about patiently encouraging your child to think about the need for a plan and allowing them to be part of that process. Household activities can help: thinking about what you're going to have for dinner, cooking, food shopping, holiday planning and banking. Involving your child will take longer in the moment but save a lot of time in the medium and long term.

'These activities can be ideal teaching tools because they have built-in incentives (you get to buy or eat what you choose, put money in the bank, or do something fun for holiday),' says Dawson. She adds that in order for it to work, you have to be engaged and available throughout the activity: 'You need to be a good frontal lobe. You can't just invite your child to join in the planning and leave her to her own devices.' Your child also has to have some decision-making power, and you'll need to gauge their interest levels, attention space and endurance. Pick a good time and wrap it up quickly if they are getting bored.

Kirstie McStay, community manager of Spectrum Gaming, a community for neurodivergent young people built around a love of gaming, is an AuDHDer and has worked as a teaching assistant. She describes her approach as 'planting seeds'. 'Some people will only do things when they've thought of it themselves, so steer them in the right direction,' she says. 'Model things, verbalise your own problem-solving thought process: "I keep forgetting to put out the bins, so I've left a Post-it note on the front door saying 'Take out bins'." If your young person is struggling and doesn't want help, tell them a story of how you had a similar problem and how you overcame it. Sometimes being told what to do is not effective or helpful – perhaps your child has to run the calculations themselves before coming to the conclusion of what an acceptable solution is.'

McStay also advises being open to what the young person suggests. 'Sometimes the only way you know if it's going to work is by giving it a go. And if it is going to fail, finding out for yourself can be more helpful. Young people can come up with some really good solutions. What is really important is to help young people understand that there are things they are going to always find difficult, because of the natural differences in the way their brains work – and that this is okay. Everyone has things they naturally find easy and difficult. Normalising the fact that people often need continuing support with things can help to nurture self-acceptance and avoid shame.'

OTHER STRATEGIES TO IMPROVE EXECUTIVE FUNCTION SKILLS

Teaching a child to clean their room

Let's take another everyday example to look at helpful strategies involved in improving EF skills. It is often assumed that children know how to clean their rooms, but our ADHD kids, as well as perfectionist autistic ones, often need more explicit teaching. Peg Dawson breaks it down into stages.

Stage 1 is parent-directed, involving you supervising your child and directing them:

'Let's start now.'

'Put your Lego in this box.'

'Put your dirty clothes in the laundry.'

'It doesn't look like all those toys will fit in one box; we'll need to get another one.'

'When you finish, you can play with your friends.'

'I know you hate doing this, but we're almost done, and when we're finished, you'll feel great.'

'Isn't it nice to have all your work for the day done?'

Stage 2 is about providing the same information without being the direct agent: the parent creates a list, a picture schedule or an audiotape to cue the child. At this stage, rather than tell the child what to do, you can just say, 'Look at your list.'

Stage 3. Parents back off more. Instead of saying 'Look at the list', say: 'What do you need to do?' By being vague, you force the child to do some of the problem-solving on their own.

Stage 4. The transfer is complete. The child looks at the messy room and decides they need to tidy it up. Let the choirs sing!

Rewards

As with everything in life, if you're doing something for the first time, or something you're not relishing, a little sweetener goes a long way towards focusing the mind. And if you really want to motivate them, ask them to come up with their own prize. Yes, you'll wince and balk if their request involves spending a large amount of money on some gaming currency – I speak from experience – but remember that the true reward, to you and your child, is a lot bigger.

How to help your child organise and do their homework

It may be helpful to make a deal with your child that at the beginning of a homework session you come up with a plan. You could write a list together, which your child fills in, with the tasks or subjects in a row and a column for your child to tick when they've done the task. As in the bedroom example above, you can scaffold the use of this form, then fade into the background when your child is regularly doing it independently.

Body doubling may help too: this is where you sit next to a child to help them focus. It can encourage them to start on a task, then you can leave once they are focused and dip in again when they need refocusing. This can be done by a teaching assistant at school, or a parent at home (I do it with my elder son, who is starting his GCSEs – I do my own work on my laptop on the sofa next to his desk while he does his home-work. I'm there if he needs me, but quietly tapping in the background if he doesn't). Why body doubling works is linked to the stimulation and dopamine hit of the company of other people (even if they aren't saying much and just tapping) that helps get the task done, combined with just having someone in your presence to help keep racing thoughts at bay, as well as gen-erally lowering anxiety. There is a whole online body doubling world, which is weird and fascinating – the body doubler joins you during a task on Zoom, which seems to work too. Now there are dedicated sites that can match you up with a body doubler, and TikTok users livestream tasks as mundane as doing laundry, inviting others to observe as a way to keep them on task.

Visual reminders

These are great for nudging things back into your child's atten-tion tunnel without having to verbally nag them. I leave Post-it notes for myself around the house all the time, including on the back of the front door telling me what I need to do before I leave. In my old job I went through a phase of sticking them to my computer, reminding me to sort out various things before I got too stressed. Colleagues eventually learnt to judge my levels of anxiety by them – if the screen had a solid border of scrawled messages, they knew to stay away!

For teenagers, you could try leaving a note on the kitchen table: *Please unload the dishwasher when you get home from school.* Do that for three weeks, and then don't leave it and see if your child gets unstacking anyway.

You can also encourage your child, if older, to set a timer or reminder on their phone, though brains of a demand avoidance variety may find this difficult, as it is too much like a demand. The bottom line is to try to limit verbal instructions, as the chances are they will just get lost in the ether or register as a nag, or they will forget what you have said within a nanosecond. This is especially true if your child is trying to get somewhere. Map, yes. Verbal instructions, no.

ADHD PARALYSIS

ADHD paralysis, also known as 'analysis paralysis', is where individuals with ADHD find themselves stuck, unable to start or complete tasks despite knowing what needs to be done. It can look like indecision or perfectionism, with a person endlessly polishing their essay and being anxious about letting go of it, or fearing having it judged.

What causes ADHD paralysis is executive function difficulties coupled with a fear of failure. Often the result is overwhelm – and sometimes, rather than risk messing up, the brain opts for inaction. Perfectionism can be a by-product of ADHD, as a child who has been told off a lot may overcompensate and become determined to never make mistakes going forward.

Signs of ADHD paralysis can include: continuously delaying the start of homework; spending excessive time planning or researching without starting the task; overthinking tasks and abandoning them halfway through; constantly tweaking an essay without finishing; hopping between many projects but not getting far with any.

What you can do about it

For these children, encourage them to focus on writing a solid first draft rather than aiming for a flawless final product. In my professional life, I have found that when I start writing a column thinking 'I want this to be the best newspaper column ever', I stop and tell myself to aim far lower. Far better to go for a non-shit column, then tweak it into something above average, possibly even good. Removing the pressure to excel means I do better work.

Breaking tasks down

The Goblin Tools website has a great page called 'Magic ToDo – Breaking things down so you don't'. For a child who gets stuck on how to break tasks into smaller chunks and what to prioritise, see if using this website helps.

I tried it out using the key words 'brush my teeth', and it broke down the task as follows:

Pick up toothbrush

Apply toothpaste to toothbrush

Wet toothbrush with water

Brush teeth using circular motions

Rinse mouth with water

Spit out excess toothpaste

Rinse toothbrush

Store toothbrush

TL;DR

A reminder of the main points of the chapter. Handy for those of you who don't have the executive function skills to read the whole lot.

- Move. If your child's brain isn't working, it may be because they need a walk, or a bounce on the trampoline.
- Focus on helping with a few EF difficulties that will make the most impact rather than trying to tackle everything at once.

- Help your child own the plan and remember: having a less effective plan that your child is engaged with is better than a more effective one you have steamrollered them into.
- Help your child understand when it's just best to quit – and that they are allowed to do this. Often young people are encouraged to stick things out, but knowing when to stop is a key life lesson too.
- For homework, see if brain breaks help your child focus. Set a timer for your child to focus for, say, fifteen minutes, then they can take a five-minute break (whether that's checking Discord, watching a five-minute YouTube clip, coming down to the kitchen for a snack). And repeat.
- Try visual clocks and timers that can show how much time left of working your child has.

But most of all . . . Encourage your child to be kind to themselves. Embrace imperfection in yourself and model that to your child. Let your child know there is no shame in asking for help when they are overwhelmed. Remind them that everyone makes mistakes and that progress and being happy is far more important than being perfect, were that even possible.

8

How to Help Your Child Be Happy

Here is a story. A dad took his AuDHD son to a museum. Knowing crowds made the five-year-old anxious, they arrived on the dot of 10 a.m. when the museum opened, and raced through the rooms so he could enjoy it with fewer people around. But disaster struck when the little boy discovered it was against the rules to go into the same room twice. He was so unhappy about it he started running about, causing an almighty ruckus. The dad and brother were mortified, the security guards alarmed and other parents judgy.

One security guard decided to take control of the situation, and loomed over the child, getting ready to tell him off. This caused something in the dad to snap. Up to that moment he had been focused on the disruption to other people, but then a single, very clear thought entered his brain: 'Fuck you all.'

And so the parent told the security guard to move away from his son, that he was making the situation worse and he needed to let him deal with it. He ignored the judgy onlookers and let his furious child run around, shouting blue murder and going back into some of the rooms they had already visited.

The dad resisted the urge to do some performative telling-off, caving in to perceived pressure to deal with the situation strictly. He knew this would have only escalated things; instead, he prioritised getting his child calm as quickly as possible.

I heard this story when I was attending a parenting group learning about de-escalation. It had a powerful impact on me, as it's the kind of situation I've been in tens if not hundreds of times with my two boys. But in these moments I rarely, if ever, have the presence of mind to realise that everyone else can fuck off, as they don't have to pick up the pieces afterwards.

This confidence to see that other people and what they think matter not one jot, and that you are the only person in the room uniquely skilled to respond to the needs of your kids, will not only help you be happier, but your child too. The story also highlights the three reasons I don't think being strict with neurodivergent children leads to happiness, or works at all.

First, being strict usually means upholding rules that don't always make sense to a neurodivergent child. In this case, the child couldn't get behind the logic of not visiting a room twice despite there not being many people there. And while the strict parenting approach is that it doesn't matter whether the child thinks a rule is illogical or not, they just need to follow it, this fails to appreciate the role of logic in neurodivergents' lives. Autistic and ADHD kids cling to logic as it helps them make sense of a confusing world. Without it, they can feel like they are cast adrift in choppy seas. While everyone needs boundaries, neurotypical children need them to be logical. Telling a child to ignore the logic of a situation, therefore, can only cause intense frustration and anxiety.

Second, we are dealing with impulsive children, and as we all know, telling ADHD children off doesn't cure their impulsivity or help them make a different choice next time – the ADHD kids in classrooms being repeatedly told off by teachers for interrupting despite their anxiety growing is testimony to this.

Third, focusing only on a person's behaviour without broadening it out to their context isn't right. The child in the story most likely wasn't only having a meltdown over a rule; the chaotic environment and the possible dysregulating impact of excitement were factors too. Focusing just on behaviour simply encourages our children to show distress more quietly; it doesn't tackle the root cause.

But if I'm honest, part of the reason I'm not a fan of strict parenting is not only for the reasons above; it's that I'm rubbish at it. I find it hard to be consistent and am weirdly bad at being in charge when I'm looking after my two boys. I have my own flexible approach to the rules that constantly appals my straight-down-the-line husband.

Even so, I believe in parenting according to your child's neurotype. And with ADHD kids this can mean prioritising your relationship with your child above them complying with the rules. One route to making your child happier in the long term is to listen and understand them, and to point out when they aren't in the wrong, they're just in the wrong environment. And when things are calm, you can talk about how you know your child thinks the rule is silly, but it can make life difficult if it isn't followed, so is there a way they can follow it next time?

But perhaps most important of all, learn to ignore the views of anyone else who thinks your child is just naughty, or that you need to be stricter. Think of yourself as the shield or the buffer between your child and external and societal pressures to be neurotypical or to behave according to the script. If you learn to ignore the pressure for your child to be so-called 'normal', they will too. And this will be the single biggest thing you can do to help them be happy.

HOW TO HELP YOUR CHILD BE HAPPY

It is absolutely possible to be a young ADHDer and have a brilliant life, but this will likely need more external input. And so as someone who loves a structured approach, I present to you my ten-point strategy for helping your child be happy.

Strategy 1: Validate . . . then validate some more

Validation is the process of recognising, understanding and expressing acceptance of another person's feelings, and we often don't validate enough. If your child is worried or upset, before rushing to distract them or coming up with a solution, first spend time acknowledging how they are feeling.

'I don't think you can overvalidate,' says Dr Helen Honey. 'It's so powerful. People worry that by doing this you will drag a child down, but it's the opposite. Sit in your child's misery and say, "I'm just going to stay with you, and we can be sad together and you don't have to talk about it if you don't want to." Then later on you can say, "Do you want me to come up with some ideas to feel better?" and if they say no, that's okay.'

Dr Honey adds that roaring into action too soon robs the child of the chance to solve their own problem – and being in possession of an ADHD brain means they are likely to be good at problem-solving. Parents can solve most problems, but it's more empowering if the child learns to do it.

How to validate someone's feelings

Give them your full attention: move to a quiet place to have the discussion and give the conversation the time it needs. Don't try to cook dinner while having the conversation – make it your priority.

Don't interrupt: zip it and focus on properly listening. This shows you care and gives you the chance to fully understand the situation, which will help you tailor your support. By avoiding jumping in with comments or opinions, the other person doesn't feel like they have to wrap up what they are saying quickly.

Ask questions: for example: 'Just to check I fully under-stand, what bit of this was the most difficult?' or 'So how did that make you feel?' or 'At what point in the situation did you start to feel like this?'

Empathise: this is the validating part. Statements like 'I would have found that very annoying too' or 'I can see why you feel that way'.

Strategy 2: Identify your child's challenges and find practical solutions together

Help your child work out what their challenges are and accept them (don't expect your child to magically be able to overcome them), and come up with practical solutions.

Andy Smith, who founded Spectrum Gaming, the gaming com-munity for neurodivergent young people, told me about the great strategies he has come up with over the years. These include going for a run when he's angry or his brain is stuck in a loop. He listens to heavy metal music and carries on running until he can't relate to the angry lyrics any more. 'I know then that I'm not mad any more and I can come back home,' he says. Mean-while, if he's struggling to write something boring for work, he takes a blank Google Doc and writes loads of swear words, which makes it easier to start the task as he's warmed his brain up by amusing it. Also, to avoid losing stuff – he has calculated that he's lost twenty-three bank cards in the past five years, and left seven games consoles on the train – he has learned he has to put his bag on his lap so he doesn't forget it. Another helpful lesson, he says, is that 'I cannot do some things until my brain says I'm ready to do them. I've got a list of 200 things that I want to do, but my brain won't let me do them yet. If you don't do this you'll always be fighting your brain and it's going to drive you bonkers.'

Other strategies ADHD adults have told me that work for them include playing loud music to help them tidy up, watching YouTube videos when they brush their teeth – motivating themselves to do an annoying, boring task by piggybacking it onto a pleasurable one.

Equally important is to identify the areas that no amount of support strategies will help and give your child permission to ditch them (e.g., if they are dyspraxic and horrible at football, tell them it's fine to avoid it even when all their friends are football mad). Similarly, sensitive ADHDers can suffer from FOMO (fear of missing out), so make sure they know they don't have to go to unstructured house parties – instead save their energy for the social stuff that works for them.

Strategy 3: TIPP skills

This is a technique from dialectical behaviour therapy (DBT), a cousin of cognitive behavioural therapy (CBT) adapted for people who experience emotions intensely. The aim of DBT is to understand and accept difficult feelings while learning strategies to manage them. It essentially gives you coping skills designed for when you've fallen into a pit of emotion and are trying to scramble out.

TIPP stands for temperature, intense exercise, paced breathing and paired muscle relaxation, and these are the things to think about in those moments when your young person's nervous system is all over the place. To break it down:

Temperature means finding a way to cool down your body. You can splash cold water on your child's face, get them to take a cold shower or hold a freezer pack on to their eyes and cheeks.

Intense exercise is what it says on the tin: encourage your child to do a few rounds of jumping jacks, run up and down the stairs, or try a quick burst of high-intensity exercises such as push-ups or burpees.

Paced breathing means slowing down your breath to about six breaths a minute, inhaling for four seconds and exhaling for six. There are online videos that can guide you and your child through this.

Paired muscle relaxation is when you tense and then relax your muscles. With your child, sit or lie down and tense each muscle group (e.g. hands, arms, shoulders, face, abdomen, legs) for a few seconds before releasing the tension and allowing your muscles to relax fully.

The basic idea is that these exercises will trick your body into thinking it's calmer – for example, the purpose of reducing body temperature is to activate the 'dive reflex', a natural physiological response that helps calm the nervous system. As mammals, if we put our faces in cold water, our parasympathetic system – a network of nerves that relaxes the body after periods of stress or danger – kicks in. As your heart rate and breathing slows, so your blood pressure decreases.

'It's an evolutionary mechanism to keep you alive when your body is plunged into water, as the brain wants you to conserve your body's abilities,' says Dr Honey. 'But then if your breathing and heart rates slow, your brain thinks it's calm. So you're tricking your brain into thinking you are calm. Beta blockers work the same way, causing your heart to slow down so your brain thinks you aren't anxious any more. If we get too stressed, our parasympathetic system isn't as active as it should be and we can struggle to relax. Some people do seem to be more prone to having underactive parasympathetic systems,' she adds. 'But if you do things like cold swimming, your parasympathetic system gets more active.'

Engaging in intense exercise releases endorphins, natural mood-lifters – do just twenty jumping jacks and your brain chemistry changes. Paced breathing and muscle relaxation further reduce stress by slowing your heart rate. But it will be a case of trial and error, since not all the TIPP skills will work all the time. I kept a cold compress in the freezer ready to soothe M's fevered and furious brow when he was in or close to a meltdown. It never made it anywhere close to his forehead, however. During one of these occasions, it ended up being ripped out of my hand and chucked at the wall.

As Dr Honey points out, however, you have to persevere until the techniques become second nature. 'It's like learning a new skill: you can't just do it when you need to, you have to practise it every day. Do it when you're feeling calm so you're ready to use it when you are upset.' For the breathing exercises, for example, she recommends trying them daily for two minutes, using a meditation app if that engages your child, though not all kids with ADHD will find this possible.

'How I'd approach these skills with my child is to say: "Which of these would you like to try first?" Usually they'll find one more helpful than another. It's about giving them a tool to manage intense emotions. I've said to my own kids, "Let's do it every day together and we'll see how we feel before and after. And once we're good at it we can use it when we get angry and upset and you can remind me which skill to use, and I can remind you."'

It's also a good idea to be aware of co-regulation, says Honey. This is the act of mirroring each other's emotions, like when you pick up a crying baby and try to soothe him or her by being calm and talking in a gentle voice, rather than shrieking, 'For the love of God, STOP CRYING!' (Though we've all been there . . .)

'It's incredibly powerful for ADHD people to have co-regulation partners, which means focusing on modelling your own emotional regulation,' says Honey. 'Keeping your response calm even in the face of highly anxious or dysregulated behaviour, for example, or doing some attuned listening (not rushing to come up with a solution on their behalf, just listening and validating their emotions) can help someone learn to regulate themselves.'

Strategy 4: Energy management

Traditional wisdom will tell you to run your ADHD kid round the garden, for teachers to let them run round the playground. But in reality, energy levels for (even hyperactive) ADHDers will fluctuate, so if your child doesn't want to run around, it's not because they aren't hyperactive. It may be that their brain has knackered them out.

'Often having an ADHD brain can be exhausting and it's helpful to teach kids about the need to manage energy,' says Laura James, a health and well-being expert and author who is autistic and likely ADHD as well. 'People with ADHD often underestimate the time and energy it will take to do a task. They will think, "Today I'll do this, go here, and write that", when there simply isn't enough time. This can be super-stressful when they fail to meet their own expectations of what can be done in a day. Plus, they often don't have the energy reserves to get through an impossibly long list so their battery gets drained. Once your child starts planning their own time, you can help by asking them: "Can you do all of these things both time- and energy-wise? Are you able to manage it all and not get exhausted? Is there a way you could plan to spread this list over a couple of days." Prioritising is important and if an ADHD child is supported in breaking down large tasks or working out what really needs to be done first, they will feel much less stressed in the long term.'

This is important, as ADHDers are very susceptible to burnout at college or university and beyond. Having a brain that is constantly coming up with ideas and pushing you to do new stuff – without always having the same skill at thinking things through and pausing to assess whether something is realistic or sensible

– means that learning to pace yourself and not fry your nervous system is important.

One tool to help has been developed by Maja Toudal, an autistic psychologist, and clinical psychologist Dr Tony Attwood in their book *Energy Accounting*. A structured approach in which energy-draining and energy-replacing activities are managed like debits and credits in a bank account, the aim is to remain in credit (calm, happy, replenished) and not overdrawn (overwhelmed, stressed and anxious). You can draw up two lists with your child: things that give you energy and things that drain your energy. The idea is that when you make an energy withdrawal from your day, you balance it up with an activity that gives you energy in return.

Strategy 5: Meditation (or a version of)

For lots of ADHD brains the idea of being told to sit still and only focus on one thought is hell (though some ADHD adults swear by it). Laura James tried classic mantra meditations and mindfulness body scans, and for her it felt impossible, like climbing a mountain. In fact, it made her exceptionally anxious. Instead, she plays meditation apps while walking, to achieve the same result but adding in the movement she needs. She also recommends guided meditations designed for younger kids and teenagers. Breathwork can be a powerful tool too: 'A simple technique such as box breathing – when you breathe through your nose for a count of four, hold your breath for a count of four, exhale slowly through the mouth for a count of four – can bring a real sense of calm to a child who is feeling dysregulated, struggling to relax or is unable to begin a task.'

She also suggests thinking of hyperfocus and intense interests as a type of mindfulness for your child: if your child is in a flow state, they are not focused on the noises in the room and everything else is tuned out (as you know full well when you're asking them to come down for dinner). Your child is not thinking 'I don't want to go into school', 'This person said this to me, what does it mean?', 'This jumper is itchy'; they are thinking of just one thing.

Strategy 6: Learn to de-escalate (think Dad at the beginning of this chapter)

We've had a tough time as a family this year, with some very big escalations (caused by adults as well as children), so I have been on a course called NVR (non-violent resistance). This is not a course designed to remind you not to thump your kids, you'll be pleased to hear; instead it is a parenting method using the non-violent resistance techniques practised by Gandhi, Martin Luther King and, in his later years, Nelson Mandela, who beautifully modelled how you can make your point without escalation.

To apply these principles to family life was the brainwave of Professor Haim Omer and his team at the University of Tel Aviv in Israel. I took a weekly seat in a draughty hall to learn more about NVR in a circle of pretty defeated-looking parents. It felt very much like I imagine an Alcoholics Anonymous meeting: a group of strangers with name badges on their jumpers sharing incredibly personal stuff. It was an experience I was dreading – I am not keen on parenting groups where you take time off work and organise childcare only for one parent to dominate it and talk at length about what is happening to them – but it turned out to be amazing.

What I've learned is that consequences like time-outs and taking away a child's screen don't work. Also, that we can't control our children, but we – parents and carers – can control our reactions.

Self-care is a key theme (which I will come to later in this chapter), along with the focus on de-escalation when a child or parent is getting agitated and a row is brewing. This usually means the parent talks less, listens more, parks their own frustrations and anxiety, remaining as calm as possible.

The 'communication model' is one technique to try for defusing rows. This involves repeating back to the child what they are saying or what you think they are feeling. For example: 'I can see you are really upset with me because I didn't buy you the Robux. You feel I lied to you and it seems very unfair' – though I have found this approach annoys my teenage son, and the advice is not to do it if it doesn't work.

The next stage is the 'deferred response' – otherwise known as striking when the iron is cold. Don't try to deal with what is happening in the heat of the moment, when your child is not going to listen to you. Wait until you're both calm to talk about what happened and how you can handle it better next time.

I have found the course really helpful, and it's giving me a framework to know what to do when my child is approaching a meltdown or things are getting out of hand. Previously I felt powerless, but now I have a plan. I particularly like the approach of brainstorming with M how we can handle things differently or avoid arguments in the future. I love the way it encourages collaboration and flexibility, and anything that does this for neurodivergent young people (and their parents) is a good thing. The rigid thinking that neurodivergent people can be prone to can make work, relationships and life generally very difficult.

Sometimes, though, I'm too tired or grumpy to apply the NVR techniques consistently. Once, before M received his diagnoses, we had an hour-long stand-off over him not brushing his teeth properly when he was exhausted. I was worried that if I backed down he'd never brush his teeth for two minutes again, but of course after our long, ugly row, we both went to bed depressed, with him having brushed his teeth for precisely zero minutes.

Strategy 7: Ditch society's norms

'So many times I've gone shopping to get food to cook and it all ends up getting wasted,' says Smith. 'I spend so long stressing about it, then decide it's not going to work. Now, I don't use normal plates. Instead I use disposable paper plates and bowls so I don't have to wash up. I also got rid of all my forks and spoons so I only have one of each. I have to clean one before I start again.' He also hates eating with other people: 'If you have to take your food from a communal bowl, I absolutely hate that. How much do I take? I don't know.'

I know an AuDHD mum who doesn't eat dinner with her neurodivergent kids and husband. She yells, 'Food is ready' and people come and get it when they're hungry, and if they don't get it when it's warm they can microwave it later. They have other times when they connect and have conversations – she doesn't feel it has to be a meal time.

Also, it is good to be aware that an ADHD young person might be more likely to question their gender. The research done so far suggests that neurodivergent people (by which I mean autistic and ADHDers) are just under seven times more likely to be gender non-conforming. We don't know why this is but some ADHDers I have spoken to suggest that if you have grown up experiencing social rejection, and having a tough time in life because you have a different brain from the majority, you are more likely to question other societal norms.

In my opinion, the approach to this for parents should be the same as has been outlined elsewhere in this book: listen, work as a team with your child to understand what they are thinking and agree together what they need from you to feel most supported. The emotions and challenges that could arise for parents of children that are exploring their gender identity are similar to those that come up for parents of ADHDers: as parents we can feel rejected or panicked if our children see the world differently to us or will take a different life journey to the one we imagined. But our job is to love them for who they are and to support them in figuring out who that person is.

Strategy 8: Accept that your children won't always be happy

One way to be instantly happier is to reframe how you define happiness. Lower that bar. Not made it through the day without completely losing your shit? Winning. We also need to lower the bar for our kids. Because happiness in the usual sense (which I am defining as an absence of above-average anxiety and there-fore a feeling of calm) is not a consistent option for most of our children going through the current school and life systems.

Lisa Lloyd, in her book *Raising the Sen-Betweeners*, maintains that we need to stop trying to force our kids to be happy, and it's an important point. I think I've been guilty of this with M a lot over the years – I wanted him to be happy so I could feel good about my parenting. But this isn't realistic, and it stopped me from seeing and acknowledging sooner what was going wrong.

We need to approach the reality that our children are likely to have some form of mental health difficulties without blaming our-selves. There are big systemic problems at work in society that we cannot solve. I can write this sentence and absolutely mean it, but also the guilt I feel – and the sense of failure associated with having kids with clinical levels of anxiety – is significant. What I can tell you, however, is that blaming yourself, which will have a knock-on effect on your kids, is a waste of your energy. We have to teach our children to go easy on themselves, by starting with ourselves.

Strategy 9: Be your child's cheerleader

Psychologists will tell you that ADHD young people need a cheer-leader who will hold the idea of the child as good, capable, likeable and worthwhile, especially when things go wrong. This is particularly true as the worst part of ADHD is the shame that accompanies it. Dr Dodson recommends saying to your child, 'I know you, you are a good person, if anyone could overcome these problems by hard work and sheer ability it would have been you. What that tells me is there is something that is getting in the way and I want you to know I'm going to be with you all the way until we figure out what that something is.' So if your child is struggling with an English task that is too abstract, too unstructured, too boring, too handwritingy, tell them it is okay that they find it hard. They can do so many other things. And this thing is stupid anyway.

Strategy 10: Look after yourself

I am not, and will never be, someone who rises at 6 a.m., does yoga, writes a gratitude journal and stares into the sun before making my kids' breakfasts. Instead, I tend to start my day in a fug of disorganisation and rising panic, as I've overslept or am racing around the house trying to find a maths book, cursing anyone who will listen for not having sorted this out the night before.

What self-care is is obvious: taking time for yourself and considering your own needs as important. I've never really seen its value, but the NVR practitioner Victoria Keverne made me rethink this when I heard her speak and she pointed out that it's our duty to be calm and not stressed for our kids. So book that massage – it would be neglecting your children not to. But also don't be a martyr. Take the opportunity for breaks, accept help from family, pay for childcare if you can afford to. And when you do get time on your own, make sure you do something for you – don't just catch up on work. Even if it's ten minutes having a cup of tea in the garden, ring-fence it. Do breathwork, stretching, yoga, go for a walk around the block. The fundamentals of being okay are eating a decent diet, getting plenty of sleep, making sure you move enough, drinking water and learning to relax. Do these things and you'll be far more resilient to the ups and downs life will bring.

Other ways I do my parental duty in this respect include anti-anxiety medication, therapy and renegotiating my job so I'm now under less work pressure but can still work part-time (thank you to my bosses, Oli, Amy and Tal).

Right, so we've covered the strategies – what you can do to help your child be happy. Next in this chapter we're going to look at the barriers to them being happy. Many of these things are connected to a societal prejudice against minority brain types that is deeply embedded in the schooling, banking, healthcare and job sectors. Basically, everywhere. But there are things you can do to mitigate all of this, as we look at below.

Barrier 1: Masking

Masking is often discussed in relation to autism, but ADHD kids mask too. Being a masker means you spend all day analysing others and copying neurotypical behaviour in order to fit in. It takes enormous energy and can cause high anxiety. My younger son, who got into trouble frequently when he first started school, used to tell me he was trying to be more like Sally, the best-behaved girl in the class. I'm ashamed to admit I was delighted, as the idea of parenting Sally seemed pretty appealing: I imagined her dutifully cleaning her teeth with the absolute minimum of nagging, having turned off the TV herself when she realised it was time for bed. But what I didn't realise was that this was a sign he was masking. I wish I could go back in time and tell him *not* to be like Sally – that I wanted him to be only him – and to realise that this was a sign he was possibly trying to lessen the amount he was being told off by the teacher. While masking can make school life easier temporarily – you get in less trouble and your classmates seem to like you more – long term it's a disaster. The mask sticks to your skin, expanding over time to cover more and more of you, to the point where you realise as an adult that you have no idea which bits are the real you and which bits are pretend.

What you can do to help with masking
Encourage your children to be their full ADHD selves at home, and avoid sending them to a school where they have to mask extensively in order not to be in constant trouble. (While there are some inclusive schools out there, there are too many with rigid behaviour rules that are doing extensive damage to ADHD pupils. This can be found particularly in some – but not all – academy schools, particularly ones where a head teacher is on £150k and under pressure to show rapid improvement.)

Have honest conversations with your child about expectations: 'I don't have a problem with you doing that, but some neurotypicals might not like it when you go to their house, so what would you do then?' Help them find compromises that don't mean abandoning who they are while being mindful of other people.

Talk about the positives of ADHD and the downsides of being neurotypical. Sure, Sally is the teacher's pet, but can she learn *Minecraft* WorldEdit as quickly as you? Hell, no. Help your child view ADHD in a more objective light, and notice as a family the downsides of being neurotypical. For example, my son was talking about how his ADHD brain made him overreact in all situations, and I asked him: 'What if your ADHD brain is right, in that it reacts *exactly* the right amount in some situations and non-ADHD people underreact?' He looked at me and smiled, before saying, 'I hadn't thought of it like that.' Talk to young people about masking and help them to recognise when they are doing it – get them to consider the cost (energy and emotion) and whether it is worth it. Tell them about an experience at work or at school where you pretended to be different to fit in, and make it clear how exhausting it was and why it wasn't a good strategy long term. How if a friend doesn't like the real you, they are not the right friend for you.

Barrier 2: Dysregulation

Difficulties with emotional regulation are seen as a key feature of ADHD. Emotional regulation is the ability to effectively manage your emotional life. To have challenges with this is to be irritable, to end up in a sobbing heap if something tiny has gone wrong, to fly off the handle or get so excited that it's a pretty unpleasant experience for everyone.

Windows of tolerance

The window of tolerance metaphor was developed by Dan Siegel, a clinical professor of psychiatry, in 1999 and is often used by therapists and professionals working with young people affected by trauma. The idea is that when we are in this window, we feel calm, we can manage our emotions, we have fun, find it easy to communicate and make good choices. But when we're pushed out of our window, we can enter hyperarousal (where the body is getting ready for fight or flight until the danger goes away, making us agitated, aggressive, controlling and anxious, feeling hot or suffering from a stomach ache) or hypoarousal (where we freeze or become very compliant, feeling foggy and discon-nected).

If a person experiences lots of stress when they are young – and I would argue that being neurodivergent will do this, particularly when you don't know you are – their window of tolerance can become smaller. Research has shown that the person who has experienced a lot of stress then becomes more sensitive to stress responses than someone who didn't experience as much stress growing up. But what I find immensely hopeful is that you can increase a person's window of tolerance. Psychologists believe the way to do this is for parents and carers to show empathy and understanding, helping our young people make sense of what they are feeling so the bad thoughts seem less dangerous to them. This involves naming the bad feelings and working out the causes, if possible; as well as focusing on our own emotional state – practising what is known as 'contagious calm' to create an environment that is as non-threatening as possible and focus on building close relationships with your child.

Medical research has put a lot of emphasis on trying to find out if and how the structure of the ADHD brain is different to that of neurotypicals and how this causes dysregulation. But I don't think enough emphasis has been put on the simple fact that ADHD people just have a lot more to be stressed about – rejection, fucking up, executive dysfunction and how much this can totally frazzle someone. It's a normal, valid response to being in a world that makes life difficult for you.

The role of sensory differences in emotional regulation
To what extent ADHD people experience sensory differences and overwhelm in the same way that autistic people do is debated, and not yet understood, but I think it's a fair guess this plays a part. Also, it is becoming increasingly obvious that a sizeable number of people who have ADHD are autistic anyway. So bear in mind that noise, light and smells could all be more overwhelming for an ADHD kid compared with a neurotypical one, which will certainly affect their ability to stay on an even keel.

If you're in a hectic, loud, chaotic place in the morning and your child is inexplicably tired or stressed for the rest of the day, it might be that the hangover is caused by the noise and commotion. If you notice a pattern, help your child make the connection between their environment and their emotional state and try to avoid overly peopley places.

Helping a child manage their regulation could include noticing when they are overstimulated (stressed out by a busy place), at which point they need to do something relaxing. But if you're seeing lots of inattention – daydreaming or not being able to get started on a task – that can be a sign that someone is understimulated, so they may need alerting activities, like some form of exercise, or using a fidget toy. ADHD people of all ages live with this tricky balancing act: trying to stimulate themselves enough to get tasks done, without going so far that they're left pacing the room. It's a bit like trying to achieve the perfect temperature in the shower every time: impossible. So if you are a parent and can help them notice what they are feeling and link it to activities that will bring them down or up, that will be useful.

Even a positive emotion can be dysregulating
Bear in mind that excitement is a difficult emotion for some ADHDers to regulate. Dr Helen Honey points out that in Buddhism, excitement, anxiety and stress are all the same thing, and for this reason she avoids situations for her son that are too exciting. 'He was looking forward to a holiday recently and it was hell for him, unbearable,' she says. 'I have a patient who gets so excited by something, he gets beside himself, it's like a torture. The natural thing we want to do is cause excitement, but maybe we need to reframe it. Titrate how much we give out.'

Dysregulated children can grow up into brilliant adults
Laura James tells me that she grew up an 'entirely dysregulated child' who never felt totally comfortable. I find it helpful to know Laura, as I know that she turned out to be a very

successful, happily married mum of four who is a brilliant friend. It is a reminder that children who have significant difficulties with emotional regulation can find ways to cope and manage their overwhelming emotions later in life.

Laura adds that when she was young, people never discussed their feelings. 'If you were crying, parents said, "Stop crying or I'll give you something to cry about",' she says. 'As parents, we have to understand that being a child is hard and being a teenager is particularly hard.' Poor emotional regulation will reach its peak in the teenage years – but on the upside, those saintly neurotypical kids suddenly aren't so saintly any more, so at least you've got a bit of company there.

What you can do if you have a dysregulated child
Encourage your child to practise with a mindfulness app, watch ASMR videos (autonomous sensory meridian response – these are videos often of people whispering or tearing paper or scalp massages that make you feel weirdly tingly when you watch them), use a weighted blanket, smell lavender oil or find other ways that help them. One teen I spoke to, Joe, a fourteen-year-old AuDHD boy who lives in London, said that when he's dysregulated he does 'online gaming, I lie down or listen to an audiobook. Other times I work out – doing the dumbbells helps quite a lot plus it benefits me.' Another young man in his twenties said he noticed that after football he was coming home dysregulated – the excitement had overstimulated him – so he makes sure he rides his bike home to help counter that.

For children of any age who are spinning out, the five/four/three/two/one grounding technique can be helpful. Think of five things you can hear; four things you can see; three things you can touch from where you're sitting; two things you can smell; one thing you can taste.

Remember, when you are suggesting a child takes steps to regulate themselves, present it like an invitation – 'Let's go on

151

the trampoline together' – rather than saying, 'You look dys-regulated, you need to do this thing.' I have to confess, despite knowing this, I'm always telling my children to go on the trampo-line because they are dysregulated and are interrupting whatever I'm doing. If M agrees, he usually does about five annoyed jumps before launching himself onto the sofa, crashing on to me and wanting to talk non-stop while I'm trying to concentrate on *Bake Off*. For the love of God, not now, Paul Hollywood is just about to give someone a handshake!

How to explain dysregulation to your child

According to speech and language therapist Natasha Hal-lam, who wrote an excellent piece for the Autism Understood website, our emotions are like an iceberg in the ocean: the visible part is our behaviour, but the bit underneath are all the things that are making us anxious and dysregulated.

Hallam explains that one of the brain's jobs is to warn us that we're in danger, so the body can do something to keep it safe. If we feel angry or worried our brain can interpret this as thinking we're unsafe – and then, 'how we behave when our brain has decided we are unsafe is not in our con-trol,' she writes.

If we are feeling anxious a lot, 'then the "smoke alarm" in our brain is going off so much and so loudly that it is constantly pushing us out of our window of tolerance and making us become dysregulated very quickly'.

The result is big reactions to what can be perceived as small triggers by grown-ups. These big reactions could look from the outside like someone who is angry, con-trolling or perhaps shut down or emotionless. Hallam writes that no one should be 'shamed or blamed' for feeling and expressing these big emotions. Instead the young person 'needs support to identify what triggers our anxiety and to create an environment that helps us feel as safe and relaxed as possible'.

Barrier 3: Rejection sensitivity dysphoria (RSD)

As covered earlier in the book, RSD is an intense emotional reaction to criticism, rejection or disappointing others (perceived or real). RSD encourages a person to mask, because it prompts the ADHDer to change the aspects of their personality that they have figured out are annoying people or pushing them away.

'I've been told, "You're so organised and good at planning",' says Kirstie McStay, community manager at Spectrum Gaming. 'The reality is I'm not, but I have forced myself to be this way because if I'm not being super organised or super helpful, then I fear everything will go bad and that feeling is crushing.'

For something to be hurtful to a sensitive RSD-prone ADHDer, it's not even necessarily about the words that have been said; it can be the tone of voice, or the sigh before speaking. Once your nervous system has decided this is a threatening situation, things can spiral out of control.

In younger children, RSD likely manifests as a tantrum, but as we get older we realise that this is not socially acceptable so we internalise the feelings, but they are just as strong. Dr Helen Honey believes that RSD contributes to a lot of the risk factors that are associated with ADHD, such as self-harm, suicidal ideation and substance misuse, as people look for ways to deal with these unbearable emotions. She adds that while ADHD medications work on the inattention, hyperactivity and impulsivity, they don't usually reduce the intensity of the emotions themselves. The exception is guanfacine and clonidine, which can have a significant impact on reducing emotional dysregulation in young people with ADHD.

What you can do to help with RSD

- Teach your kids about it. 'Knowing about it really helps – then when it happens, the child can speculate if they are feeling that way because of their RSD,' says Dr Honey. 'It's important for the child to know this is a thing and that others have it too.'
- Normalise your child asking 'Are you mad with me?' – model it by asking it of your children. Society can view seeking reassurance as needy, but it's really about gaining useful information and nipping things in the bud.
- Offer reassurance to your child when you get tetchy. Explain that you used an annoyed voice because you are tired, not because you're upset with them.
- Remind your child when they are feeling RSD that the feeling won't last for ever. They've felt like this before, it's horrible, and it will pass.
- Tell your child about a time you messed up at work or school and got told off because you weren't as organised as you ought to have been. Explain that while initially you felt ashamed, you then realised it's human to mess up and you're still a good person, so you decided to go easy on yourself.
- Bear in mind that masking to avoid rejection takes a lot of energy. So if your child is exhausted a lot of the time, consider if this is a factor.
- Come up with a plan for when RSD rears its head, something distracting or self-soothing. Keep a box full of sensory toys to hand, or things like essential oils that your child can sniff to help calm the nervous system again.

Barrier 4: The subtle signs of trauma that may not be recognised in your child

For hyperactive and impulsive ADHD kids, masking often involves joking and messing around – in short, playing the class clown. As a result, teachers can look at the child and see an extrovert, someone funny, disruptive and confident. The tomfoolery can hide someone far more vulnerable, however.

Pete Wharmby, a former teacher turned author who is autistic and has ADHD, points out that class clowning can be a trauma response. Most of us know about the fight-or-flight reflex in response to trauma or danger – children in fight mode may appear angry all the time, while those in flight mode will be seeking to escape a situation – but there is also freeze (when they go into shutdown) and fawn (going into people-pleasing overdrive). The fifth trauma response beginning with F is less well known: funny.

If you make people laugh then, you might think, they won't hurt you and you can make them like you. 'You are doing this to stop people being unpleasant to you or traumatising you further,' says Wharmby. 'And if you are struggling with neurotypical social skills, it may be one of the only ways you know to get people to like you.'

Since realising that my son often finds himself trapped in the final F, I can no longer watch the films of the comedian Jim Carrey, who was diagnosed with ADHD and dyslexia as a child. The last time we were on a family holiday, we put on one of his biggest films and I found it almost unbearable. There he was, investing every ounce of his being – and getting progressively more over the top as the film went on – in getting laughs. The title of the film? *The Mask.*

The ADHD adults I've spoken to for this book talk about playing a role either to get people to like them or to minimise bullying – they became the feisty one in the class, the funny one.

Andy Smith from Spectrum Gaming says that some of the young people in his online community can get annoying when they are anxious – they stop listening and deliberately do things that are frustrating to others. 'When I'm terrified, I put on an act and can be overconfident and boisterous,' he says. 'When I was at university, I didn't speak to anyone for quite a long time. When it came to the time that you had to move in with people, I didn't have anyone to flat-share with, so I forced myself to go to a party. I drank a lot and put on a performance, and the next day I was asked to move in with people.'

What you can do to help if you have a mini class clown
- Concentrate on increasing the support for your child, as they may be experiencing social difficulties, and speak to the teacher and SENCO about your concerns.
- Be very clear if you feel the driver behind the behaviour is high anxiety and masking, and speak to the school about getting a referral to CAMHS to see if they can help.
- Try to speak to your child about it, and if they find direct conversations too difficult, tell them about times you felt awkward and worried that people didn't like you so you felt this pressure to be entertaining, and how it left you feeling.

Barrier 5: Teachers, the world and us parents not recognising ADHD anxiety

I went along on a school trip with M's class as a parent volunteer (say what you like about having a lively ADHD kid, at least you know that when you stick your hand up to help on a trip to the zoo, you'll be the first one picked!). Aside from seeing how hilarious and kind kids are, what I noticed was that when neurotypical children show anxiety or distress it often gets attended to, but when neurodivergent pupils do the same, it often gets missed.

I found it upsetting to see the teaching assistants gather round a neurotypical child who was crying because she was scared of pigeons when there was less consolation for the dysregulated ADHD girl having rows with her peers throughout the day. Similarly, there wasn't obvious support either for the autistic kid who had been isolated from their peers all day and was tuned out and quietly stimming. It's not that the lovely school staff don't care: the reason they don't respond to these little distress flares being sent skywards by the neurodivergent kids is that they don't see them. And how could they, when no one has trained them up properly, thanks to the local authority or government not funding or prioritising good-quality training given by neurodivergent adults.

Parents don't always see them either – at least I didn't. I made the mistake of assuming my son was confident when actually he was a world away from it. He was the Jim Carrey of his class, masking his distress with jokes and horseplay and telegraphing his anxiety by getting more and more 'out there'. I later realised I was attuned to spotting neurotypical or autistic anxiety, but not ADHD anxiety.

What to do if you are wondering if your child is anxious rather than extrovert (or both)?

- Carefully observe your child and ask them, in those moments when they are particularly 'extra', if their heart is beating fast and their body feels jittery.
- Once you notice what their anxiety looks like, and how they communicate it, feed this back to the school, with strategies you have found helpful.
- Talk to your child about anxiety: help them recognise it themselves and give them strategies to lessen it (it may be needing a quiet space, to listen to music).
- Discuss when you are worried and how it makes you feel and what you do to try to feel less worried.

Barrier 6: Online gaming (though I'm not so sure it's a barrier at all)

My kids are online a lot and I have mixed feelings about it. As I'm writing this, it's lunchtime and my nine-year-old is playing *Minecraft*, and has been since the moment he woke up. I'm in no doubt online gaming is regulating my two and helps them recover when their social batteries are drained after school or a rare foray beyond our front door. I'm doing something not dissimilar also: my husband works at the weekend, so the boys and I have 'lazy Saturdays', which took shape because I couldn't cope with single-parenting my neurodivergent lovelies after a full-on week at work. On those days, we're all largely on a screen and unable to face the world. I used to feel embarrassed about these lazy days, that it wasn't 'right' to be indoors when we should be having outdoor experiences. I would also suddenly get cross with the boys for not coming off their screens the moment I wanted them to – the anger driven by my guilt at having allowed them so much time online in the first place.

But now I feel that allowing ourselves recovery time is part of energy management, which is a vital skill to learn. Still, I do want more balance in our lives, things to do on a Sunday that involve exercise and, crucially, that my boys will buy into. So I'm trying to find things we can add to our lives.

My husband and I have different takes on this, and we argue about it a lot – he thinks we should regulate their screen time better, that they should get far less than they do, and not that I tell him this, but sometimes I think he's right. I wish I could say I have an approach that I am confident about all the time, but I confess I feel torn and feel different things at different times.

We have had some brilliant help from CAMHS while M has been off school, and one valuable lesson I've learnt is that instead of expecting a child to come off a screen abruptly, it's better to try spending time with them when they are on it, engaging with the game they are playing. Take an interest and learn about it, then discuss together coming off it and see what a difference it makes. In general, it pays to understand your child's online world. Get an account and play *Roblox* or *Minecraft* with them. I try, but I'm so bad – I can barely walk straight, which amuses my children no end.

It's not only a case of if you can't beat them, join them. You should get involved because this is where your child is spending a lot of their time, and why wouldn't you want to be a part of it? That way if they are having trouble with friendships or being bullied, it's far easier to talk about it. You'll also see how good they are at certain things.

'Online gaming can be a problem in a person's life, but it usually isn't *the* problem,' says Andy Smith. 'When young people are gaming non-stop, it's symptomatic of them struggling, and they are using gaming as a way to cope. Some of the people we support are out of education and in burnout. They don't game for fun, they game because their self-esteem is so low it's all they have to feel good about themselves.'

Smith believes that online gaming doesn't get enough credit for improving kids' social confidence and being a sandbox in which to practise building relationships. 'I made my first friends on the internet when I was being badly bullied at school,' he says. 'In the online world I had friends to speak to, where my presence felt meaningful. I learned a lot of life skills in the games: how to problem-solve, strategic planning, and I could learn these things in a safe environment, where it doesn't matter too much if you get it wrong.'

It's possible that if a child is really stressed a lot of the time, screen time helps to regulate them. Being pulled away from that abruptly is likely to cause a big reaction, which is when parents may find a young person is argumentative or aggressive. This can make it look like it's the game causing the behaviour when it may be the underlying issue, such as spending too much time in a classroom, leading to sensory overwhelm and dysregulation, and in fact the game is helping to bring that young person back to balance. It's also true that screens are bloody hard to come off, as I know thanks to my shameful nocturnal *Candy Crush* and Instagram habits.

Spectrum Gaming as an organisation argues that gaming itself doesn't make people more prone to depression. Instead, it's a tool that they believe depressed and stressed neurodivergent people are using to make themselves feel better. For this reason finding out what is overwhelming that child is a better course of action, rather than demonising screens and removing them without establishing the underlying cause.

'What can help is to work with the young person to find different regulating activities, then add in more opportunities to do that activity instead, which will gradually lead to a decrease in reliance on screens,' says McStay. She adds that it's better to add the new thing first and to focus on increasing that, rather than to start by removing screens in the hope that your kids will be forced into using another regulatory tool or strategy.

You can work together to find other activities that give the same level of satisfaction, releasing dopamine and those happy feelings.

A mother's view on supporting her ADHD child to be happy

It was not always easy to get Millie to understand society's nonsensical neurotypical rules, so we changed the shape of things. For example, if we went out for a meal in a restaurant, she would run around. So one of us would get up and wander around and find things of interest to her. We would order a variety of things and silently swap meals

---

we had ordered so that she could eat her desired choice. Other parents thought we were spoiling her, but I knew we were giving her what made her feel peaceful and safe inside and we were also investing in our day as a family.

We felt profound judgement from other parents who assumed we were pandering to Millie's needs. It was about making sure she was understood and heard. I would invest and prepare so that I knew the next time we went for a meal, she would know it was going to be okay. She would know Mum would make sure the food was right.

At bedtime, as a child she needed certain routines to happen: the bed had to be made a certain way, with the blanket on the bottom, the bunny on her pillow. I wasn't indulging her, I was comforting a child with specific needs. It was all those little tweaks and investments that made the night-time routine calmer and smoother – which is very important.

As a family, now that Millie is a grown woman, we still invest in her calm and peace. She recently had to go to hospital for an operation, so I just shut my business and went to London to sit with her. When I arrived to meet her, she was refusing to go into her room and the nurses were concerned that she was not going to be able to be left alone. Her autistic traits came to the surface and she presented as still vulnerable and totally dependent – even as a now doctor of bioinformatics, an award-winning writer and incredibly well respected in her field. She needed me by her side as she went into shutdown.

This is what mothers do, I know this, and I would do it all again in a blink of an eye, but it is not 'typical' parenting – in many ways she is for ever a child. Eventually at the hospital, Millie was able to process events and came around and began to behave like a mature young woman. But she is often masking. She'll go home and regress, and her partner understands that about her.

I still often end up as her first point of contact in situations that are complex or difficult to navigate. Millie can still find it hard to connect with any other person's needs outside of her own. Due to Millie's heightened sensory needs, whatever the temperature in the house is, it has to be right for her. Is there hot water for her bath? Is there an electric blanket on her bed? Recently, I have tried to pull back and think about how she's a grown woman now, and it's not all about Millie's needs. Having said that, I am very aware that Millie experiences the world in a heightened sensory way. I can't change that, so as a family we accept it.

Over the past decade, things have improved considerably, but Millie, like many young adults, will ring because she needs me. She'll start the conversation with: 'Hi, Mum, how are you? What have you been doing?' And then, within seconds, it's: 'So this has happened, how do I process it? What should I do? And this has happened, and I can't deal with this any more.' And it's an hour long. We help keep her balanced. But then, however, especially during a family crisis or illness, Millie can step up like no one else, with data and constructive advice and knowledge. She is the most fragile but also the most fiercely intelligent and resilient human I know.

Sonia Pang, mother of Camilla Pang

TL;DR

If you have taken anything from this chapter, make it these points.

- Validate your child's worries more than you currently do – this means not leaping to a conclusion, or interrupting but empathising and properly listening to what they are saying.
- Identify challenges and come up with practical solutions . . . also, help your child learn the things that they will never be able to do easily and teach them it's okay to give these things a hard pass.
- Teach your child about energy management: yes, all these plans sound amazing, but do you have the time and energy to do it all?
- Think of hyperfocus as a time of meditation or mindfulness for busy ADHD brains.
- Learn to de-escalate when a row is brewing with your child, and focus on communication and the relationship with your child in those tricky times, knowing you can tackle whatever the issue is when things are calmer.
- Look after yourself. This is essential: you can't help your child be calm if your own nervous system is fried.
- Be aware of masking and teach your child they don't have to do this. Why be someone else when they can be themselves?
- You can help your child increase their capacity to be calm and regulate themselves by focusing on keeping calm in the face of their dysregulation and helping them return to calm more quickly.
- Be aware of rejection sensitivity dysphoria and normalise your child checking in with people to see if they have offended them.

- ADHD anxiety doesn't always look like neurotypical anxiety – it can present as someone acting as a class clown or seeming boisterous. Too often in schools the behaviour is seen as disruptive rather than anxious.
- The most important way to help your child be happy is to take the time to understand them and to lessen the shame associated with growing up an ADHDer in a neurotypical world.

9

Negotiating with Your Local Authority

I have been putting off writing this chapter partly because it's hard to explain the laws and rules around the support your child is entitled to in school as it's an opaque and legalistic system. But also because I feel I messed up getting help for my sons in different ways, and it especially stings when I think about my younger son, whose support at school wasn't right for years or possibly ever, despite the fact that his mother had written a book on the importance of getting it right.

And then I get annoyed because people like me – parents and carers – are often left with the burden of feeling like we've failed our kids when really it's the government and the systems that are meant to be helping us that should be carrying the guilt.

Thanks to the media articles on this issue, a small proportion of which I've written, you'll probably know this is a system in crisis, a system that denies children their legal rights because central UK government hasn't given local government enough money. Local authorities now routinely break the law, and the Department for Education turns a blind eye as it can't afford to acknowledge the issue. For too long it hasn't been a high enough priority – far easier to blame the crisis on pushy parents like you and me rather than the department's many failings.

This chapter is designed to give you a broad idea of your child's rights and the issues you are dealing with. I have negotiated

Education, Health and Care Plans (EHCPs), the legal document outlining what support a local authority has to provide at school by law, for both my sons after it became obvious they needed more support than the school could fund. Both times it's ended up with me doing 90 per cent of the work, causing big arguments with my husband as I feel resentful over the stress I'm taking on, while my husband has a wife who is flying off the handle and who is being a micromanaging control freak when he does get involved.

The stress is high because I feel powerless. I am having to be calm, polite and reasonable – and remain persistent – while I negotiate with a system that is close to broken. And because of this, you have to be clued up, but no one can simply describe the process in one sitting as there's too much to know. So you have to spend large amounts of time you don't have training yourself in the law and learning a new bureaucratic language as well as trying to work out who best to email, what to say and at what point to start getting assertive. It's like a high-pressure manage-ment job, but the stakes are far higher than any job as it's your child's happiness on the line. Oh, and you have to do all of this in your spare time on top of your normal job, as you also need to still pay the mortgage while supporting your child who is in crisis, which is why you're getting an EHCP in the first place.

But dear God, don't let me put you off. Local authorities – as well as schools – have a lot of responsibilities around children with special educational needs, so the people who persist and won't be fobbed off are generally the people with children getting more appropriate support. So empower yourself with knowledge and go for it. Read up about the law on the website of the legal charity IPSEA (which has good template letters to download for specific situations) and the website Special Needs Jungle. Because no matter how hard the negotiations are, and how-ever tempting it is to hide from the situation because you can't face dealing with it – which is what I did with my son – it's not as hard as watching your child's happiness be destroyed by a lack of support at school.

HOW I NEGOTIATED MORE SUPPORT FOR MY SON

I decided to write a timeline of my efforts to date to get my son an EHCP. But then he stopped being able to go to school, so it also charts our (likely) move from a mainstream school to a specialist one, negotiating with the council to pay for a tutor to come to our home while he's out of school along the way. These negotiations are still not resolved, so sadly there is no neat ending for me to report to you. I am aware that launching into the timeline, which outlines some of the processes I'm involved in, might get confusing, so to begin with I've done a flow chart that hopefully will make the system clearer. Although I think it is inevitable that I will confuse you – it's a lot of information to absorb – please bear with me and hopefully by the end of the chapter you'll have a solid overview. The flow chart is just the process; I will explain how you tackle the steps in the process later on in the chapter.

The SEND flowchart of bureaucratic doom

Your child has special educational needs, otherwise known as SEND. They may have an ADHD diagnosis, or are being assessed for ADHD and need support to keep focused, organise themselves and integrate socially.

They are put on **SEN support**, which is the lower level of support for SEND children. In theory, schools have up to £6,000 per child with SEND to spend on their support a year (and this isn't dependent on the child having a diagnosis, it's dependent on need). If the school provides support and your child is making good progress, then you can stay on SEN support. But if the school says they can't afford appropriate support for your child, or more support is needed above the £6,000 threshold, you or your school need to apply for an **Education, Health and Care Plan (EHCP),** which is the higher level of support.

You or your school do this by requesting an **Education, Health and Care needs assessment.** Your local authority (LA) has six weeks to give you an answer as to whether it will carry this out or not.

If the LA says yes to a needs assessment, it has sixteen weeks from the point you request to carry out the assessment. But the far more likely scenario is that your LA will say no, at which point you can appeal the decision, by requesting **mediation,** which is a formal meeting to discuss why you disagree (sometimes these meetings are helpful, other times they aren't and just delay things further); or you can skip this and go straight to the **SEND Tribunal,** where a judge will look at the evidence and make a legally binding decision.

In terms of the time scale for an appeal, you have two months after the LA has made its decision to go to tribunal (after this point you lose the opportunity to do so), and you must have considered mediation. This doesn't mean you have to go through mediation, you just have to have a **mediation certificate** from the service. If you don't want mediation, you call the mediators and say you're not doing it and they will send you a certificate. You have one month after receiving the mediation certificate to take your case to tribunal.

The LA agrees to carry out a needs assessment. An educational psychologist will automatically be involved, but you can request other professionals to assess your child, such as a speech and language therapist or an occupational therapist.

If after the end of the needs assessment the LA says no to issuing an EHCP and you still think your child needs one, you're back to mediation and/or tribunal to argue why they should have said yes. If, however, the LA agrees to issue an EHCP, it must send out its **draft Plan** to be reviewed by you, the parent/carer, before it is finalised. This is your chance to say what you think is missing, points that may or may not be included by the LA.

The LA issues a **final Plan**. If you don't agree with the contents – or the school setting – you can go to mediation and/or tribunal.

The EHCP is reviewed each year in a meeting, at which point you can add to or amend its contents. After every annual review, your right to go to mediation and tribunal is opened again, with the same timelines applying: two months after the Plan is finalised post annual review, or one month after you have received a mediation certificate.

THE TIMELINE OF MY THREE-YEAR NEGOTIATION OVER SUPPORT FOR MY SON

September 2022. M has a speech impediment, so I ask the school to request an NHS speech and language therapist (SALT) to assess him. She responds to say she is not concerned about the impediment but refers him for an autism spectrum condition and ADHD assessment. She tells me that he appeared highly dysregulated during the assessment. The SALT signs him off as he doesn't have problems with speaking, 'only' social communication. He is put on the SEN support register at school, meaning we have termly meetings about his support.

Early 2023. M is diagnosed with autism spectrum condition (with demand avoidant features) through the NHS, ADHD and developmental coordination disorder (DCD, previously known as dyspraxia) privately. He is assessed by an occupational therapist (OT) from the local authority – a key professional who can help him with focus and manage his ADHD in the classroom. The OT, SENCO and I have a brief and confusing Zoom call after the assessment in which I start to doubt the OT is actually talking about my son, but before I can clarify, the call ends, cutting us off mid-conversation. It was later confirmed that the OT had indeed mistaken M for another child on their caseload. Seven months later, I get a letter from the OT saying they have assessed M, he's being signed off. I'm too angry and dejected to reply, which I later very much regret.

September 2023. M is clearly miserable at school. There's a general deterioration in his self-esteem and happiness. We commission a private educational psychologist (whose role it is to identify barriers to learning and suggest ways to remove them) to go into the school, assess him and write a report, which made very difficult reading. In November, I ask for a six-month sabbatical from work, as I think that if I can be around more and liaise with the staff, he may be able to remain in school.

December 2023. We apply to the local authority to carry out a needs assessment for an EHCP. We give them our private educational psychologist's report; a report from CAMHS, who have been working with us since M was referred for an ADHD assessment; a private OT report; the report from the aforementioned SALT and the ADHD and ASC diagnoses report highlighting pronounced difficulties with focus and anxiety. We also say that we think there is a possibility of school refusal on the horizon if he doesn't get increased support.

February 2024. The LA rejects our request for the needs assessment, saying that M can be supported in the school under SEN support. We register an appeal with the SEND Tribunal. To apply, we filled in some simple forms that we downloaded from the government's website arguing that our LA came to an assumption without providing any evidence that it had looked into whether the school could afford to meet M's needs without an EHCP – which we emailed to the tribunal courts. We requested a paper-based decision (rather than a hearing we attend in person), in the hope it would speed things up.

I speak to our local SENDIASS (Special Educational Needs and Disabilities Information Advice and Support Service), which is free and independent, though funded by our local authority. Every LA has one and ours has been brilliant. The manager there, Davut, says he will raise our case with the council. He emails me to say they are taking the case back to what's known as 'panel' – a meeting of senior people in the SEND department and SENCOs from schools where such decisions are made. It's all very secretive – no minutes of their meetings are ever published, nor do parents know exactly who is on the panel. I imagine a cabal of people in hooded capes meeting in a dark room like they do in the TV programme *The Traitors*.

March 2024. M stops being able to attend school. We get an email from the SEND Tribunal giving us a date for a decision in July. A week later, we receive an email confirming that the panel has decided they will do a needs assessment after all, and they email the tribunal to say they are conceding. We ask them to assess M for potential OT and SALT needs – both departments refuse to do this as they say they have already signed him off. I curse myself for not rebutting the earlier report from the OT department.

April 2024. The council's educational psychologist (EP) assesses M at home (the LA always has to send an EP to assess a child as part of the needs assessment process). She says that getting him back to school is going to be hard and notes he's still very anxious about school and can't talk about it with her.

May 2024. The local authority issues a draft Plan, which details a lot of need and outlines the interventions the school needs to implement while giving them the lowest level of funding and no external professional input – such as occupational therapy and an overview by a specialist autism teacher. The Plan assumes M will magically return to school without providing the school with external help to make this happen.

June 2024. We have a 'co-production meeting' with our LA case-worker (the person who oversees the paperwork on behalf of the council and compiles the evidence to panel) and the school and we say what we think is missing, which is, among other things, reasonable funding and external professionals feeding in.

July 2024. Very little is taken on board from the co-production meeting and the Plan is finalised still with the lowest level of funding and no professional input supporting the school. Meanwhile, the school is going to huge efforts to support M back – teachers are visiting home, writing notes to him, and we're having lots of communication with the SENCO, but it's not working.

I talk to the caseworker at the local authority about the lack of OT and get frustrated with her, even though she is clearly doing her best and is straightforward with me. I then feel bad as I'm shooting the messenger. I later apologise to her, and she thanks me. She says her job often involves managing complaints and 'there's not much joy'.

M has not been in school for four months, and there has been no learning. I send a formal letter of complaint to the LA over M's lack of education, pointing out that they are not fulfilling their legal duty, that he has had no suitable learning and that the chances of him returning to school are lessening by them not addressing the growing learning gap. The LA start paying for a mentor/tutor to come and work with him two hours a day. The tutor, Huseyin, specialises in working with kids who have had negative experiences of school – he is amazing and spends a month building a relationship with M and getting to know him while going out for milkshakes and playing fun games on his laptop before slowly introducing maths. For the first time in four months, M is starting to engage with someone other than his parents. We feel hopeful.

August 2024. I request mediation and say I want to discuss the fact that the provision in our Plan is unspecified – particularly time with the teaching assistant – when by law all provision set out in the Plan has to be specified. I also request OT, SALT, and support from a specialist autism teacher, which I think is necessary to integrate him back into school. I ask for the work he's been doing with CAMHS to be specified in the Plan – CAMHS offered him weekly therapy sessions, but although he's been unable to engage, hopefully in the future this will change, and I don't want the offer to vanish. I've commissioned a private OT report (at a cost of £800) to evidence why he does need OT, which again makes difficult reading. It outlines very significant sensory needs and recommends a specialist school placement.

September 2024. M is about to join Year 5. He's expressed a desire to return to school and the school has put a teaching assistant in the class who he likes. He lasts for twenty minutes before the 'bad feelings return'. He's not been back since. We have a review meeting with the LA, and the professionals and the school express the view that a mainstream environment no longer looks suitable for M given the level of adult support he needs and the flexibility. I haven't heard back from the LA with a response to our request for mediation, so I email the head of SEND at the LA, and they agree to enter mediation with us.

We have mediation, which is a Zoom call with a kind mediator, our school SENCO, and a caseworker from the council. I tell the LA we have an EHCP that can't be implemented as it assumes M is in school. Since he isn't, he's not receiving any of the provision on the Plan. It was suggested the school should hold an emergency annual review of M's EHCP, during which we can make a request for a special school placement, which will then be considered by the panel. This is due to happen in mid-November. I had spent easily five hours writing a document detailing what I felt needed to be added to his EHCP that ended up not being used. I come out of the meeting feeling like I've been run over. I find it hard to string a sentence together.

October 2024. Huseyin, the tutor working with M, recommends a school where he used to work for M. I speak to the head, who tells me that their focus is on building up young people's self-esteem and rebuilding a more positive relationship with learning. This seems perfect, though the placement at the school, known as alternative provision (schools that kids who can't go to mainstream attend), will be short term, with the plan being to transition him to a suitable school once he's in a better place for learning. At the time of me sending this book to my publishers, the issue is unresolved, but I'm feeling hopeful. All the professionals are on the same page and having a plan at last is helping me feel calmer. The worst-case scenario is we have to go to tribunal in a year's time to resolve it if the LA doesn't agree to the alternate provision. The thought of M being isolated for another year is difficult, so I'm choosing to think positively and not second-guess everything. It's a process I can't control, so I'm trying to expect the unpleasant twists and turns.

WHAT SUPPORT YOUR CHILD IS ENTITLED TO AND HOW TO GO ABOUT GETTING IT

The timeline above highlights the difficulties, but also hopefully it shows you that you can do it. Essentially the tribunal service is your friend and you should not be put off using it. Government data shows that parents win their cases 98 per cent of the time (evidence that decisions around support of kids like ours are consistently unlawful up and down the country), so it's a no-brainer. LAs tend to be poor at providing evidence to support their position, so if you are able to gather your own (via minutes of school meetings, professional reports, etc.), you have more than a fair chance if your request is reasonable.

While so far in the chapter we've been taking a high-level look at the process, the rest is now the nitty-gritty: how you actually go about getting the support your child is entitled to. Some people who have the money pay for a lawyer – and some who don't but who can't cope with the pressure any longer or have a terrible LA who simply won't play by the rules unless they are forced to – do too. We did this when my elder son needed a specialist school for secondary. It cost us £20,000 all in all, with the council conceding everything just before our date in court. Some people do spend less on legal fees, though – it depends what is involved and how many professional reports you are getting. But I'm hoping to outline the ways people who can't afford lawyers can still get appropriate support for their child. If I can help popularise people using the tribunal service – where judges make an effort to support those who aren't using lawyers and where parents are virtually guaranteed to win, given that councils are only successful 2 per cent of the time – it will be a life well spent.

What are the different levels of support?

As we've covered, there are two levels of support that children with special educational needs receive at school: **SEN support** and **Education, Health and Care Plans** (EHCPs). SEN support is generally for kids whose support needs are lower, and it costs the school below £6,000 a year (the amount the Department for Education – the DfE – gives schools per pupil to support children with SEND). EHCPs are for kids whose support costs over this threshold, or if the school says they can't pay for reasonable interventions the child needs.

It's important to know that while this £6,000 threshold is commonly used by LAs, as it's part of the funding arrangement between schools and the DfE, it is not a legal threshold. A judge at a tribunal won't care how much the school is spending; their only concern will be the legal definition, which is that a) the child or young person has or may have SEND and b) it may be necessary for special educational provision to be made for that young person in the form of an EHCP. As you can see, it's a low bar to meet, which is why almost everyone who goes to tribunal saying their LA should have carried out a needs assessment wins their case. It's also important for parents to know that in theory, schools have £6,000 to spend per pupil with SEND without the need to get an EHCP. Schools will usually say they don't actually have this money, but that's a conversation between them and the LA; it's not your concern. If a school says it can't spend money on support your child needs, you or the school should request a needs assessment for a Plan.

Provision of SEN support – what might this look like?

A teacher may have to differentiate lesson delivery; the child might need sensory toys or a standing-up desk. Or they might need flexibility on what the lesson objective or outcome is – this could mean filming an interview with a peer, rather than having to write a long answer. The school should also take advice from professionals when needed (e.g. involving an occupational therapist and educational psychotherapist to identify difficulties and come up with strategies); and include small-group work if necessary (e.g. handwriting classes). There may also be some support during the school day, perhaps at play or lunchtime; training for teachers or other staff; supported social opportunities (e.g. *Minecraft* or Lego lunchtime club); staggered lunchtime break to avoid busy times; differentiated homework (e.g. using a computer to create a poster rather than having to draw one).

In terms of meetings, schools are under a duty to have an early discussion with the pupil and parents about extra support. According to Barney Angliss, a former SENCO and consultant in SEND, this should look at desired outcomes, and what the steps are to achieve these outcomes. 'A clear date for reviewing progress should be agreed and the parent, pupil and teaching staff should each be clear about their roles,' he says.

177

How do I make a request for a needs assessment?

If your child isn't making good progress under SEN support, or it's obvious from the start that their support needs will necessitate a Plan, it's time to request an EHCP. To do this, the school fills in a very long form (the cynics among us may feel that LAs deliberately try to bury busy SENCOs in paperwork in order to make applying for a needs assessment as unattractive as possible). If the LA agrees to the assessment, they will send out an educational psychologist to observe your child, who will make recommendations that will form the basis of the Plan.

What is an Education, Care and Health Plan?

The EHCP is a legally binding document that states what support the local authority must deliver, backed up by a budget. Parents can request a school to be named as part of the Plan that they think is suitable for their child – if it's a state school, you don't have to live within the catchment area. It also doesn't have to be a state school; it could be a private school, either mainstream or special. Essentially the LA can suggest what it believes is a suitable school, but you should do your research too. If you are requesting a LA-run school, they can disagree with the placement if the school feels it can't meet your child's needs.

What is included in an EHCP?

The Plan contains eleven sections – below is a summary of each. For more information on what the Plan should contain, IPSEA has produced a comprehensive document explaining the sections and what should be in each (on its website, ipsea.org.uk). The main thing about Plans is that they are legally binding and the support detailed in them has to be specific. LAs will often try to keep it vague, so they can change it or not provide it more easily, but this isn't what they are meant to do. So, for example, section F needs to be clear about who is delivering the provision, and how long for: don't accept 'regular speech and language therapy' (Halley's Comet is observed regularly, but this only happens every seventy-two to eighty years). Instead, it needs to be stated that it is four sessions a term carried out by a speech and language therapist one-to-one for forty-five minutes a session, including some time spent in the playground observing what is happening there.

A – Views, interests and aspirations of the child or young person. The parent writes this if their child is young or pre-speaking, involving them and reflecting their views.

B – Special educational needs. What your child needs at school to progress.

C – Health needs. Your child's health needs, which are related to their SEND.

D – Social care needs. Your child's social care needs, which are related to their SEND.

E – Outcomes sought for the child. A set of short- and longer-term objectives that the EHCP is trying to achieve and the steps towards meeting them. Outcomes that will prepare them for adulthood should be linked to their aspirations in section A and should link up with the needs identified in B and C and the provision required in F–H.

F – Special educational provision. This lists the support provided to help with the needs identified in section B.

G – Healthcare provision. Health provision to be provided by the NHS. This can include support and therapies, such as medical treatments and delivery of medications, nursing support, specialist equipment and wheelchairs.

H1 – Social care provision. Any support that your child needs in accordance with section 2 of the Chronically Sick and Disabled Persons Act 1970. This might include practical assistance in the home, adaptations of the home, help with travel and 'facilitating the taking of holidays', non-residential short breaks (these are day trips run during half-term or holidays to give parents a break) and any support the parent may need.

H2 – Social care provision. Any other social care provision reasonably required to help with your child's development, e.g. residential short breaks and 'services provided to children arising from their SEN but unrelated to a disability'.

I – School placement. The name and type of school or other educational setting to be attended by the child or young person.

J – Personal budget. How much the LA will give the school. Also, direct payments to parents to cover the support detailed in the EHCP if the local authority is not paying directly (for example if your child is happily working with a private OT, you may request for this arrangement to continue and the LA to fund it).

K – List of advice. The advice and information gathered during the EHCP needs assessment must be attached here.

The key parts of the EHCP

Sections B and F: special educational needs and provision

It is important to have all your child's educational needs identified in section B. Every special educational need in B must be matched by provision in section F. Basically, if the provision isn't nailed down in section F it may be hard to enforce.

LAs sometimes try to put SALT, OT and physio in section G (Health) rather than F, meaning it is the responsibility of the NHS, whose budgets are even more squeezed than local authority SEND departments. This will make it much harder to enforce.

Sections H1 and H2: social care provision

This bit of the EHCP rarely happens. LAs are allowed to take into account the cost and convenience of providing social care – something they aren't allowed to do for provision laid out in section F. And even if you do get provision included, it is delivered by notoriously understaffed social service departments. Most people don't have the stamina to sort out the social care side of things as well as the education component.

Section E: outcomes

What the SEND code of practice says about outcomes:

EHC Plans should be focused on education and training, health and care outcomes that will enable children and young people to progress in their learning and, as they get older, to be well prepared for adulthood. EHC plans can also include wider outcomes such as positive social relationships and emotional resilience and stability.

An outcome can be defined as the benefit or difference made to an individual as the result of an intervention. According to the SEND code of practice, outcomes should be SMART: specific, measurable, achievable, realistic and time-bound. Outcomes can follow from the aspirations identified in section A, and should be the guidelines for what the EHCP is hoping to achieve – a combination of short-term goals (the next one to two years), medium term (end of the current school phase) and long term (when your child is twenty-five). A lot of LAs want to keep outcomes short term so they can argue that if those goals are achieved, then the need for the EHCP has come to an end, so make sure there are medium- and long-term goals in there too.

There is no limit to the number of outcomes you can specify.

Some examples of good outcomes, provided by the Council for Disabled Children:

By the end of Year 9 William (twelve years old) will be able to make his own way to school every day.

By the end of KS1, Sheila (six years old) will be able to express her preference when offered a choice between two activities.

Mason (four years old) will be able to engage in a play activity that he enjoys with another child and an adult on a daily basis by the time he is in reception.

When should you apply for an EHC needs assessment and what should be in the application?

If your child needs more support than the school can provide from its ordinary provision, then it's time to apply. Hopefully the SENCO will have gathered some good-quality evidence around what the school has tried and what hasn't worked – and having a professional report (by an educational psychologist or a speech and language therapist) boosts the likelihood of an LA agreeing.

One of the many injustices of the system is that an experienced SENCO may have a far better success rate of getting needs assessments approved than an inexperienced one, as they may provide their evidence in a clearer way or know what the LA is looking for. Below are some of the things that will increase your chance of success, in the hope that you can collaborate with your SENCO to build a persuasive case.

The evidence from the school should ideally take the form of an 'assess, plan, review, do' cycle of interventions detailing what has been tried, how it was delivered, how often, what the outcome was and how these outcomes are different to someone who doesn't have special educational needs. Alongside this, it's helpful to have the minutes from meetings with parents, school and professionals discussing what hasn't worked and why. Context is important. If a report states that a child can focus for ten minutes, but that can only happen with one-to-one support in a room with no distractions, those details must be very clearly noted. Heba Al-Jayoosi, an experienced SENCO working in London, says that when she submits a request for a needs assessment she includes a table detailing what that child can do in a small group, what they can do in the whole class and what they can do with one-to-one support, to make it really clear. As an example of evidence for a needs assessment for a seven-year-old with dyslexia, she might include details of a reading recovery intervention (which has a good research base) that has clearly been well implemented and carefully tracked by a qualified teacher. 'So in the application for the needs assessment, you could say: we carried out this programme for twenty weeks and the pupil only progressed to level 3 when we would expect a typically developing child to have progressed to level 17 over the same period of time. They have also failed their phonics test and we have done a dyslexia portfolio – a 45-minute online assessment – and here is the data.'

If you give vague information without an evidence base, this may be questioned by the LA. For social difficulties, Heba Al-Jayoosi recommends including information about the evidence-based language interventions that have been tried: for example, Talk Boost or Talking Time – if these haven't worked, you can argue more successfully that a child needs something more individualised. 'What an intervention is meant to do is level the playing field – it's meant to help the child with SEND make accelerated progress, so if this doesn't happen, then more or different support is needed.'

With ADHD, she adds, it is harder to evidence specific interventions because there aren't many with a solid evidence base thanks to a general lack of research in the area. 'What can be helpful is if an educational psychologist does an assessment of executive functioning, as this can clearly show a child's problems with working memory and impulse inhibition and they can spell out the impact this has on a child's work. I would follow it up with examples of their writing, which is something ADHD kids often have difficulties with: here is an example of a typically developing child in Year 2 without support; look at this ADHD child's writing here when it's unaided and look at what it is with support, when allowances are made for their sensory profile. But in order for us to get to the latter, we needed X, Y and Z. The school will also need to make clear that the improved writing happened during a timed intervention and it's not financially sustainable for the school to carry on providing it unless the school receives extra funding.'

In order to evidence spend of more than £6,000, Al-Jayoosi does a costed provision map with every needs assessment request to lessen the chance of it being knocked back. 'If I'm suggesting that a child, for example, needs one-to-one support for three hours a day, I won't just put down the salary for the teaching assistant for those three hours, I'll put down the educational psychologist's time required to assess the child and brief the teaching assistant on what they should be doing with the child, the time the TA needs to make visuals (say two hours a week), the OT sessions that are needed as well.'

She adds that in her school she has some children 'where they just cannot sit still even for two minutes on the carpet, and their behaviour is putting them at risk of exclusion because the impact on other children is high, so I emphasise that in the application, or if the behaviour is putting themselves or other children at risk, or if they are at risk of "school refusal" – which means they cannot attend school because of very high anxiety. These are things the local authority will take seriously, so we will detail if a child is disengaging from school and parents are finding it increasingly hard to get them to go in. If there isn't other evidence, that would be my focus.'

What to do if your request for a needs assessment is turned down

Go for mediation or straight to tribunal (though at the time of writing there is a wait for tribunal hearings of up to a year, so many people will try mediation first in case it is helpful). I only know of one parent whose child had their needs assessment request agreed the first time round. I think it's reasonable to assume that the majority (perhaps vast majority) of requests are turned down first-time round, as a way of minimising demand and costs. For the parents who persevere, in almost all cases the LA will have to reverse its decision eventually at tribunal. The legal threshold for an LA agreeing to an assessment is low, so keep going. Often this whole process is one long negotiation, so don't assume you've had a final answer on anything until you've exhausted all options (contacting your MP, making an official complaint on the council's website, etc. – as ever, though, make sure you have a valid concern to complain about rather than something minor).

Can you apply for an EHCP if the school doesn't want to?

Yes – you can email the LA SEND team (you should be able to easily find the main SEND email address for your LA on Google) with your request and evidence. I did it this way just to try to spare our overworked SENCO from filling in a huge form for the LA. If your school supports the application it may be easier to convince the LA, but if you have good evidence (most likely in the form of a professional report) it's still possible without the school.

The value of professional reports

Professional reports are a key part of your negotiation with the local authority, and are very helpful during any mediation or tribunal process. An educational psychologist, who will identify barriers to learning and suggest strategies that need to be in place to remove these, will provide vital evidence. If you can afford a private EP report, that might be something to consider – we have worked with the fantastic Ruth Birnbaum, who has advised us on suitable schools. I have always found it very help-ful having someone neutral (not paid for by the local authority) to go in and objectively say what support a child needs and what the reality is for that child at school, a picture that can be worse than a parent realises (or better).

Not everyone will be able to afford a private report, but whether you are working with the LA EP or commissioning your own pri-vate report, Barney Angliss recommends asking them to use the assessment tool known as BRIEF2 (behaviour rating inven-tory of executive function, second edition). This will report on a child's ability to: resist, or not act on a thought or an impulse; self-monitor their activity; regulate their emotions; get started on a task; keep information in working memory to help sustain attention on a task; plan and set goals; organise ideas; check the accuracy of their work and organise the things they need.

'This will suggest strategies and interventions for children with ADHD, making it a useful planning tool for schools and colleges,' Angliss says.

What if you know your child needs support but you can't afford a private report?

A professionals meeting (also known as a multi-disciplinary meeting) is the name for a type of meeting where professionals from different departments gather, and they can be very helpful for evidence. If three professionals are concerned about something – one of those can be you, the parent, and another the SENCO, and maybe someone from CAMHS, or an educational psychologist – then you can provide the minutes of that meeting to the LA as evidence.

Is it okay to wait?

Parents frequently get the message from the local authority that waiting is okay when it isn't. 'I recommend not waiting any longer than is needed to gather sufficient evidence so the application is less easily bounced back,' says Al-Jayoosi. She adds that with ADHD, Plans can take time to be agreed, as the difficulties may be initially viewed as behavioural problems by the school and LA; also because of the delays caused by the waiting lists at CAMHS to get a diagnosis. 'If we think a child may have ADHD and they are struggling we may ask the educational psychologist we work with to assess them and write a report rather than wait for a diagnosis from CAMHS, because it is quicker.'

Some schools pay for private educational psychologists to assess a child so that they can include it with the request for a needs assessment, but not all schools have the budget to do this. Head teachers also view it as wasted money, as if the request is accepted, the local authority then sends out their own educational psychologist to assess them anyway.

Do you need to worry about annoying the LA and whether this will mean your child gets less support?

It's got to the point where if parents are not assertive, their children won't get what they are legally entitled to. Senior people in local authorities understand the law, and it's likely they know that they're breaking it, but they can't do anything else because of their dire budgets. 'From the conversations I've had with managers of SEND departments, they know parents are just asking for their legal rights, so I don't think parents should worry about annoying them,' says one SENCO who didn't want to be named. You can also bet they would be asking for the law to be met if it was their children who needed support.

What to do if the needs assessment happens and the LA educational psychologist's advice is vague

The LA EP's recommendations will form the basis of the draft Plan. While some EPs employed by the LA do thorough reports with specific recommendations, others do not, as there is pressure on them about what they can and can't include in their reports because of budget constraints. The EP will show parents their report before it goes to panel, so you can discuss any points you disagree with then. Once again it will be helpful if you have evidence, in the form of other professional reports, or a report from the school, to back up anything you say.

'If I was a parent, I would insist on a cognitive assessment, because those are standardised assessments that can't be argued with,' says Al-Jayoosi. 'Sometimes an EP working for the

LA will say, "Well, I'll do a quick observation, and I'll write some advice", but I would push for the full assessment, because LAs have thresholds that the results of these assessments can trigger: e.g. if progress is two years below where a child should be, then the LA may be likely to agree to a needs assessment. The SENCO can then say: 'Here are your thresholds, and this child meets them.' If your LA won't budge and amend the Plan, and you feel the EP has underplayed your child's struggles and as a result they don't have adequate support, the next stage for the parents is mediation; then, if that doesn't work, tribunal.

What is mediation and how does it work?

People have mixed experiences of mediation. Some have found it helpful, particularly those who can produce new evidence in the form of private reports for the LA to consider. Others have found it to be a waste of time, and sometimes LAs don't even respond to say if they will engage with it or not. No matter that they have to by law – as usual, no one is there to enforce this other than frazzled parents. If you don't hear from your LA thirty days after requesting mediation, the mediators will automatically issue a certificate, which means you can go to tribunal.

The mediation sessions usually happen on Zoom and the mediator gets in touch before the meeting to discuss how it will all work. I have just done this for the first time and it was pretty baffling, with the process very poorly explained by the mediation service, but we did find it helpful for two reasons: one, someone senior from the SEND department joined the meeting (and now seems to be involved in our case); and two, we agreed an emergency annual review to re-examine the EHCP. This annual review restarts the whole process, so you can apply for mediation and tribunal two months after the negotiations with the local authority around the review are completed.

Tribunals

You have the right to appeal the decision of the LA in relation to a child's or young person's EHC needs assessments and EHCPs; this will be heard by the Special Educational Needs and Disability Tribunal in England and Northern Ireland. In Wales it is the Education Tribunal for Wales; in Scotland the Additional Support Needs Tribunals.

Tribunals are made up of a judge and usually two experts in education and special educational needs. They generally take place on Zoom (before the pandemic they were in person). The process is meant to be as user-friendly as possible, and you don't need a lawyer, so don't be intimidated out of doing it. The judge will only consider the law, not local policy, nor whether a local authority can afford your child's support (though the cost has to be reasonable). They will weigh up the evidence given by the local authority and the parents and come to a decision ten days after the hearing.

As mentioned, there isn't much downside to going through this, other than sacrificing your time and blood pressure. However, at the time of writing, there is a waiting list of up to a year, though new judges are being recruited to try to address this, and priority is given to children transitioning to primary school, secondary or college. The upside of the process is the local authority has no choice but to start playing by the rules. We went to tribunal over the school placement for my elder son – the LA had placed him in the local secondary comprehensive against the advice of his primary school and all the professionals involved. The local authority conceded the case ten days before our tribunal date, but only after we had burned through thousands of pounds. Who needs savings?

What you need to apply for a tribunal

1 Form 35 from the government website (the Application for Appeal form), which is a simple form giving your address, your child's name and the reason for appeal.
2 The decision letter from your local authority saying they have turned down the needs assessment request or have finalised your EHCP.
3 The mediation certificate, showing you have completed mediation, or don't want to pursue it (it won't affect your case if you turn it down, but with tribunal cases taking twelve months to happen, more people are considering it).
4 All the evidence you submitted to your LA with the assessment request.
5 Any other documents you think are relevant.

Email all of the above to send@justice.gov.uk, typing NEW APPEAL in the subject line.

What to expect at tribunal

An online hearing will appear much like a business meeting or work call rather than what you see in courtroom dramas. The judge will lead the hearing.

Practical tips to help you prepare for the hearing

1 Make sure to give any witnesses advance notice of the date and time of the tribunal and that everyone has the login details if it's on Zoom, and to test out the link an hour or so before your tribunal is due to start.
2 Make sure everyone who needs to have the 'Tribunal Bundle', including any witnesses, has received it. You should have received a copy of this from the LA – make sure it's in front of you when your hearing happens.

3 Make sure you're not in a noisy room and that you won't be interrupted.

4 Have Post-it notes on the pages where your key evidence is found. It saves time searching for it if you can name the bundle page number and go to it immediately, if needed.

5 Tempting as it is, try not to interrupt anyone. Have a piece of paper to hand so you can write down any counter points you want to make when it is your turn to speak.

6 Have a clear idea in your head as to what issues need to be discussed and agreed, so you're able to give a coherent summary at the beginning of the session if the judge asks for it. Tie any point you make with evidence you have to support what you are saying – it may be easier to have a list of the key points from the evidence you have to hand so you can easily find it in the moment. Practise what you are going to say with a friend beforehand.

'I watched my son in the playground, sitting alone, while all the other kids were with their friends.'

My autistic son is nine now. He'll be ten in December. He attends a specialist private school and it was a horrible fight to get him there. I first started the conversation with my local authority around his support when he was going to school at four. The caseworker's main priority, I thought, was to keep cost to a minimum. She told me he would be fine in a mainstream school without an EHCP, despite him not being able to speak and still wearing nappies. I was naive, and I thought she would advise me correctly. Of course he gets to the school and they quickly told me they couldn't meet his needs and he needs an EHCP and a specialist school. I used to see him in the playground at that school, and he would just be sitting on his own, and all the other kids would be playing and doing what they're doing, and he would just be sitting. I cried myself to sleep many, many times, because I just thought: how am I going to get out of this situation?

Around this time I was working as a PA to the head teacher of a mainstream primary school. As part of this job I saw what support other children were getting and learned about the process and the funding. It was absolutely devastating to discover I had been so badly misled. I think being a young working-class black mum meant I wasn't given the information I needed. I worry for parents who can't speak English where there's a language barrier and things, because I know they're not given the correct information.

During the pandemic, when schools were shut, my son's mainstream school told me that he couldn't attend because they couldn't keep him safe even though the prime minister stated children with SEND should attend school. I decided to speak with my MP, but while I couldn't speak to him, I met with his advisers, who were helpful. They sent a lot of emails to the Department for Education and the council, and helped me with my housing situation.

After a lot of stressful negotiating, the local authority eventually placed him in a private specialist school. It's a really lovely school that understands him. I'm so pleased with how he's coming along. He's still trying to communicate with us. He's partially verbal at the moment, and is learning to read. I think he might have some dyslexia, but there isn't enough verbal communication back and forth yet to assess him. But I mean he's thriving. My focus is on him being happy and being in the right

*school that understands his needs and can support him
every step of the way. I wouldn't have been able to get
through this journey without the help of my family. My
auntie Gen who is like a second mum to me and my mum
have been very supportive and I cannot stress enough
how important it is to have a strong support system when
you're going through something like this.*

Shanelle

TL;DR

How to get the support your child is entitled to in ten bullets.
You've got this.

- There are two categories of support at school: Sen support
  and an EHCP.
- Schools are in theory obliged to spend £6,000 per year on a
  child with SEND under SEN support. If the school can't spend
  this and your child needs more support or their support costs
  are higher than £6,000, it is time to apply for an EHCP.
- An EHCP is a legally binding document outlining what support
  a local authority has to fund at school.
- Local authorities are under pressure to reduce the number of
  EHCPs they agree to (while often cutting support at school,
  which drives people to need them – go figure).
- They often use unlawful local practices to say no to assessing
  for an EHCP.
- Parents can challenge the decisions of local authorities at the
  Special Educational Needs and Disability Tribunal. Those that
  do win 97 per cent of all cases.

- Don't hesitate to appeal any decision at tribunal – you don't have to have the experience of a lawyer to undertake this and chances are you will win your case.
- Often local authorities concede just before tribunal, and may take your case more seriously.
- Gather your evidence, be persistent and read up on your child's rights (the responsibility is on local authorities to support children with SEND).
- Don't give up; you can do this. It's stressful but not as stressful as sending your child to the wrong school.

"I watched my
son in the playground,
sitting alone,
while all the other kids
were with their friends"

10

Support at School

Tadpole-gate happened in 2019. M was three and had just started nursery, and one morning he arrived to find a rectangular tank sitting on a table, filled with water containing nine tadpoles. Next to the tank was a bowl of earth. I assume the theme of the table was nature and children were invited to watch the tadpoles as they grew into frogs, and to touch the earth.

Except my son M and his lively friend did more than touch the earth and peer at the tadpoles – they chucked the earth into the tank. At pickup time, the frustrated nursery teacher told me what had happened, and informed me that after removing the earth, they could only find six tadpoles. The accusation was floating in the ether: M and his friend had killed three tadpoles.

Trying to make amends, I told the teacher I would find three new tadpoles. After WhatsApping friends to work out where the hell you found them, I ended up dangling over a stinking algae-covered pond behind the school, jar in hand, catching no tadpoles.

And then I stopped trying. I was done trying to make amends for a situation that in my mind was stupid. Still to this day I don't know why there was a bowl of earth next to the tadpole tank, practically inviting a child like mine to commit tadpolicide. Of course my son had no intention of killing the tadpoles; he was just impulsive. And this would not be the last time that this part of his ADHD – this part of who he is – would get him into trouble at school.

The remaining two years at nursery – connected to my children's mainstream school – didn't get any better. Neither we nor the teacher knew he had ADHD and consequently a lot of his behaviour was seen as naughty. He was described as 'silly' a lot. At one stage he was sent to the head teacher (he was three).

When I dropped him off at nursery for the first time, I was certain he was a confident, non-anxious child with a large personality (when the kindly nursery assistant bent down and asked him what he wanted to do on the first day, his response of 'painting – and no singing' delighted me).

But having ADHD – and worse, undiagnosed ADHD – meant he was unable to conform to the school's behaviour expectations. Over time, the repercussions left him anxious, and depleted his self-esteem. In retrospect, it's clear he was never as bulletproof as I thought, as the assessment processes that accompanied his diagnoses of ADHD, ASC and DCD highlighted the likelihood that I wasn't recognising his anxiety and dysregulation.

But as painful as my nine-year-old's nervous breakdown has been, it has come with upsides. It has forced us to make efforts to understand him and pulled me out of my complacency. I quit my demanding job – I couldn't continue in front-line journalism, ignoring what was happening at home because I was too busy for it.

I don't blame the nursery teacher, even though I wish she'd behaved differently: the council-maintained nursery isn't funded properly and my own lack of curiosity around what was really going on didn't help us get to the bottom of things.

Schools haven't yet developed the knowledge or the strategies to properly support ADHD learners. Too often the problems faced by ADHD kids are framed as ones relating to poor behaviour, or their mental health. If you were to look at M's EHCP and professional documents, you would see his primary need listed as mental health. But this is rubbish. His primary need is to go to a school that works for his ADHD brain and doesn't constantly stress him out. The mental health outcome was the consequence of this need not being met. So it wasn't just innocent larval amphibians paying the price.

This chapter comes in three parts: practical strategies to discuss with your school; how you can work best with the school so these good ideas are actually implemented; and what to do if things go wrong. This way you can hopefully avoid a tadpole-gate situation in your own family.

PART 1: PRACTICAL STRATEGIES TO HELP YOUR CHILD AT SCHOOL

Suggestions for ways to get the support right at school for your child, and make learning appropriate for their brains. To be shared and discussed with teachers and tried out at home.

Movement and brain breaks

ADHD kids need more movement and stimulation to focus. The dysregulated and understimulated kids will be the ones annoying their teachers and peers by tipping their chairs back, clicking their pens, distracting friends or staring out of the window. One remedy is regular movement breaks, ideally carried out every fifteen to twenty minutes by the whole class – they can be as simple as a teacher putting on a song for two minutes for a dance break. The idea is that students get a brief rest from what they're doing and dopamine from the burst of exercise, which will help them with executive function and general focus. AJ, a ten-year-old with ADHD living in London, describes what it's like being stuck in a classroom when you hate being still, when all your energy is taken up by not moving, leaving little left over for learning. 'It makes me sad that I can't move around when I want to. I always want to move around and when I can't I don't listen to the teacher.'

Allowing stimming and fidgets

Every classroom should have a basket of fidgets. Fidgets shouldn't be called toys as really they are focus aides: they help keep a busy brain engaged. Some teachers think that if a child is 'playing' with a fidget toy then they can't be listening, but the opposite is true: by not allowing them or removing them at the earliest possible moment, teachers may be preventing pupils from engaging with their learning.

'I'm an adult and I use fidgets in meetings or when I have to concentrate as they keep me stimulated,' says Jess Wilson, senior SEN officer at MindJam, the online mentoring service for neurodivergent young people. 'People assume fidgets are there to occupy your hands, but it's actually more about what they are triggering in your brain,' she adds. 'No one fidget will cover all your sensory needs – sometimes I need a fidget that clicks because I need that audio output. Other days I like a hard squish, but other days a soft squish is better as you don't need so much resistance, and you're after something gentle.'

Wilson likens her attention to a balloon. 'I need it to stay tied down to something – for example a fidget – or it will just drift. It's not an intentional drifting, and I won't even be aware that I'm doing it until I look back. When this happens, I'm like, "Oh, everyone's still there, but I've gone." Fidgets and movement are ways to keep you physically in the room.'

Stimming and any in-the-seat movement that doesn't distract other pupils should always be allowed. 'Stimming is simply a coping mechanism to deal with stress,' says Pete Wharmby, an

AuDHD former secondary school teacher who now gives talks on being autistic and having ADHD. 'For autistic kids, stims are usually responding to external stimuli; for ADHD kids they are responding to internal stimuli, like a constant feeling of restlessness.'

Make sure the child knows it's really okay to use the fidget toy

It's not uncommon for a parent to be told a child can do X and Y, but the child is too scared to actually do these things as they worry they might get in trouble (particularly in light of the rejection sensitivity that is so common in ADHD). 'It hasn't been fully explained to them, or there is inconsistent messaging because one teacher will allow it, when another doesn't,' says Wharmby. 'And if they are autistic as well, they'll obsess over when you're really allowed to do it.' Ask the teacher to make it explicit to the pupil that they can use their fidget toy or whatever has been agreed, and in the beginning, invite them to do it.

Work with special interests

ADHD pupils will most likely have strong interests or passions, so if teachers can relate tasks to a pupil's special interests as much as possible, this can only be a good thing. Special interests can bring great joy in a neurodivergent person's life. In ADHD they can be replaced more frequently than they are in autistic pupils, which means a teacher may need to keep on top of what the special interest is for the week, and not assume it isn't a special interest because it is relatively short-lived. A teacher who is prepared to work with a child's special interest will build trust with neurodivergent pupils, who may well be more likely to confide in that teacher.

ADHD

Give ADHD kids more than one thing to do at a time

Sometimes concentrating on one thing at a time can be anxiety-provoking for the ADHD brain, as there isn't enough of interest there to focus them. Also, flitting between tasks is something an ADHD brain does naturally, so if your child can do this at their own pace, it is far easier than expecting it to stay on task with one topic.

'In my own life, I will scoot from doing ten minutes' writing, then a bit of social media, then watering the plants,' says Pete Wharmby, author of *Untypical*. 'I'm flitting through these tasks in quick succession as this is how I work best.'

Create a menu of tasks

Even better is to provide a menu, which gives the ADHD pupil choice and autonomy. 'Some teachers give kids a menu of tasks, which can be done in any order, an approach that is often reserved as a treat for end of term or when the teacher is tired, but for ADHD kids this kind of approach is incredibly valuable,' says Wharmby.

This technique was popular when he started teaching in 2007. In his first job in a girls' grammar school in Lincolnshire, there was an experienced teacher who championed it. 'She would give pupils a list of tasks and they were each worth a different number of points. The expectation was that by the end of the term, you would have done X number of points' worth of work, but at your own pace. It was brilliant, but then, to be blunt about it, the Conservative Party won the election in 2010 and everything changed. By the time we got to 2015 or 2016, you would get annihilated if you tried it. And now, of course, we're seeing the impact of that, because an increasing number of autistic and ADHD kids can't attend school any more. The focus is on teachers talking, no group work, no flexibility. And ADHD and autistic kids need flexibility to go in different directions.'

Understand executive dysfunction

Schools punish pupils for forgetting homework, not remembering their pencil case, wearing the wrong uniform. Detention can be the consequence, based on the assumption that you can remedy forgetfulness. But no amount of detentions will stop an ADHD person forgetting their stuff.

'You can't cure executive function difficulties by trying harder,' says Jess Wilson. 'Instead these children need to learn they have a need for support in this area. Tasks involving executive function will be hard, it's not them being lazy. ADHD pupils may struggle to get going – task initiation – and chances are they're feeling bad because everybody else is ahead and they're behind.'

In terms of what schools can do to help kids with executive function, the research and practice in this area is still developing, but adult support is usually necessary. Someone to check in to see if the child is getting on with the task okay. Perhaps they need help starting it, or just something to keep them focused (possibly a deadline: 'How about five minutes of work, then you can do ten jumping jacks?'). Another thing the child is likely to need help with is breaking down the task into manageable chunks. Remembering multi-step instructions may not be realistic, so don't give a long verbal explanation. Presenting things visually can help pupils, particularly if they are autistic too.

Normalise a child zoning out or finding it hard to focus

Expecting a child with inattentive ADHD to not zone out is setting them up to fail, so allowances must be made for this being not only a reality, but part of a child's learning style. The shame of not having consistent focus is not to be underestimated – an ADHD child will most likely think this is a by-product of them not trying hard enough, when actually it's to do with their brain.

'If a teacher says, "Oh, I think you might have zoned out, which is fine, we all do that", that can be enormously powerful,' says Wharmby.

Be prepared to explain things more than once

Related to the point above, it's inevitable that ADHD kids will regularly miss a teacher's original point, or an autistic pupil will misinterpret it. Yet in classrooms there is this Victorian belief that everything has to be heard and understood the first time and children can be made to feel bad if they fail to do this. 'Most people in conversation waffle and overexplain, and one reason we do that is we want to minimise the amount of information not being received,' says Wharmby. 'But teachers have got this weird thing where "I've said it once, and that should be enough." You wouldn't do it in business, would you, because of all the predictable problems it would create. Pupils should be allowed to ask clarifying questions.' Teachers also need to be aware that if a task isn't explained logically and very clearly, it may be confusing for pupils who are also autistic.

Understand what ADHD productivity looks like

'In ADHD pupils you'll see bursts of productivity that put neurotypical students to shame, interspersed with periods of lower effort and low energy, or what could be viewed as "messing about", Wharmby adds. 'When I was a teacher, I would be very happy for an ADHD kid to do a really quick burst of work, and then read for a bit or doodle for a bit, or even, you know, get up and tidy the classroom, as long as they aren't distracting others.' More recently, productivity experts have focused on how the key to productivity isn't discipline – it's joy. This is a notion that is relevant to ADHD brains.

Barney Angliss, a former SENCO who is now an adviser in special educational needs, adds that ADHD pupils are much more likely to have an 'exploration' approach to learning and decision-making, which involves trying out new options that may lead to better outcomes in the future. 'They might spend time digging around among scraps of information – some of it relevant to the task, some of it much less so – rather than spending time putting the information to practical use in order to complete the task,' he says. 'This is why life feels so unproductive with ADHD and why children and young people with ADHD often experience school and college as exhaustingly frustrating, because when they become interested in something and start to scavenge other pieces of the information puzzle is usually the moment when they divert from the teacher's plan. For students without ADHD, they are likely to experience the satisfaction of a finished product because they will select, focus and plan so much more efficiently.'

Adapt the environment

My son had an Eiger standing desk converter, which meant he could stand up and sit down when he wanted. It is brilliant – a wooden platform that sits on the normal school desk and the height can be adjusted. Some schools also use inexpensive cardboard dividers that can be placed around a child's desk to minimise distractions (failing this, seating an ADHD child in a place that has limited distractions is helpful). Visual timers that the teacher projects onto the whiteboard can help focus too: knowing there's a deadline to how long an activity will last can make it much easier for students with ADHD to stay engaged (but bear in mind that timers can make some students anxious). For all adaptations, a good approach is to make the less expensive ones available to all kids so as not to stigmatise anyone.

Deal with things in the moment

ADHD people can live in the moment, which has implications for support at school. If a child is upset, asking them to write it down then discuss it with a parent or teacher hours later is no good; it needs to be dealt with then and there, and if an anxious ADHD child is not able to do this, their learning is likely to be affected.

No way can you do that!

Challenge accepted. Some ADHD kids can find challenges extremely motivating, so if your child is younger, suggest to the teacher they try acting dumb and say, 'I was going to give you this task but I don't know of another X-year-old that has completed it, so I'm not sure whether to give it to you now' – and see what happens.

Eat the frog

Mark Twain once said that if the first thing you do each morning is to eat a live frog, you can go through the day with the satisfaction of knowing that it is probably the worst thing that is going to happen to you all day long. (Not all of my books contain this much frog abuse, I promise!) In more modern times, eating the frog has become synonymous with doing the hardest, trickiest job first. For older ADHD pupils who have more choice about the order of work they do, encourage them to do the most difficult task first, to avoid procrastination.

Rewards/motivations

What someone else thinks is important is unlikely to be particularly motivating to your child, and the stickers and ClassDojo rewards that work for neurotypical primary school kids are less likely to encourage a mini-ADHDer. This is certainly true of my son, whose class reward system was to get pieces of paper praising them for displaying a good learning habit. When I fished one of these crumpled pieces of paper out of his school bag that had clearly been there for a long time, I made a big deal of it, only for him to stare at me sternly and ask why I was making a fuss about a piece of paper. And I'm not sure the tea with the head and deputy head, who are often there in a disciplining role, is quite the treat for ADHD pupils that the school thinks it is either. For a reward to be motivating for ADHD pupils, it's best to ask them for ideas, or offer options.

Use music

Music can be helpful for focus if it can drown out distracting sounds, or keep someone on track. 'I use music to help my students motivate and stay on task,' ADHD coach Leslie Josel wrote in *ADDitude* online magazine. 'I have them create a "study soundtrack" – a 30- to 45-minute playlist of music they love. The key is to use the same playlist every time they sit down to work. Eventually the music will act as a motivator; when they hear the music, it sends a signal to the brain that it's time to get work done. Playing the same playlist every time they sit down to work eliminates the distraction of changing songs.'

She also encourages students to choose songs they know well so they don't get too focused on the music itself, and to make a playlist for different subjects or for shallow or deep work. Audiobooks can also be brilliant. They can be more engaging than traditional reading, with the narrator's voice keeping the listener's interest for longer. The bonus is you can do other things while you listen: tidy your room, jump on a trampoline, go for a walk or try to fall asleep. 'It can be magic for people who don't like staying still for a long time, and also can help motivate a person to do the boring jobs,' she adds.

207

Keep things moving

Tasks ideally need to move fast for quick brains, or a person may disengage and get bored. I have ADHD friends who love audiobooks because they can listen to them at 1.5 times the normal speed to help keep them focused. In a similar way, I have another friend who loves rugby but never watches the game live. Instead, he watches it afterwards, changing the settings to double speed.

Provide frequent positive feedback

'Before I realised I was neurodivergent, I had diagnosed myself with social anxiety,' says Kirstie McStay. 'I was really worried what people were thinking of me, whether I was messing things up, how I came across when I was talking, whether I'm weird, whether I laugh too much. Then I discovered some home movies of me at the age of between six and ten, and I was just constantly told to stop being silly. On one video, I asked if I could play on the slide, but my dad said "Yes, but don't be silly." And on watching it, I thought: "It's a slide – how do I go down it silly?" It was constant corrections all the way through. If your existence is incorrect and wrong, of course you are going to struggle.'

There is no doubt that ADHD kids get far more negative feedback in their lives compared with neurotypical ones – both from peers and adults. Catching ADHDers when they are good can help balance things out. My son's wonderful Year 4 teacher labelled him 'the Tech Guy' and would call on him in class to help with all things computer related. M loved this, and now if anything happens with the TV or laptop, he says sternly, 'Mum, they don't call me the Tech Guy for nothing.'

Giving ADHD pupils opportunities to be successful and do what they are good at as much as possible is also very important. Academic kids get so much positive feedback for being clever; kids with learning differences often not so much. I'm certain that if teachers could swap brains with an ADHD pupil for a day, they would realise the Herculean levels of effort needed to concentrate when you don't have easy access to dopamine, and would be praising them all day long.

What school was like when I was young – by adult teachers and educators with ADHD

'I had to hide how unfocused I was'

I was a secondary school English teacher for thirteen years. When I was a kid at school, I was well behaved and petrified of criticism. I couldn't let the ADHD win, if you like. I couldn't be hyperactive, and had to hide how unfocused I was. I remember vividly sitting quietly in lessons while everyone was working around me and almost having to stuff my fist into my mouth to stop myself from blurting something out or getting up and running about. The effort required to not do these things meant I didn't get much learning done. My legs would be going like billy-o – it was just nervous energy, and I'd be doodling all the time and struggling to listen to the teacher.

I got through it, but it was hard. There was a period at primary school when I was frequently being sent out and told off. I remember feeling constantly anxious and the teachers being confounded by me. I was popular with them because I was conscientious, outwardly very chill, and quite talented in some things, but they sent me out because I couldn't shut up. I have very strong memories of being in Year 4 and it was a terrible year, and then I managed to get the ADHD under control. After that I was never sent out of the classroom again. But managing to get some control over it came at a price, because I was having to mask intensively and focus so much on stopping myself from acting out that I couldn't focus on the work. As a teacher I had constant and debilitating trouble with marking books because it was so repetitive and I couldn't focus. I can only do so much of something boring.

Pete Wharmby, AuDHD former secondary school teacher

'If my teachers knew I had a PhD in education, they would never believe it'

I hated school. After getting my diagnoses – I'm autistic and have ADHD – it makes sense why. I was one of those bad kids, so dysregulated. I got arrested and was suspended. I barely scraped through secondary school. If I went back to my teachers now and told them I have a PhD in education, they would not believe it. But not everyone's road is linear; sometimes people take the scenic route, and the beauty of the world we live in now is there is flexibility in terms of when and how you do things.

**Jess Wilson, senior SEN officer at MindJam,
an online mentoring company**

'My teachers were baffled I got the grades I did'

I grew up in a small community in Australia and back then it would have only been boys who displayed very obvious physically challenging behaviours that would have been identified. I was a precocious child but I was severely bullied in primary school. I had no friends and I hated going – I used to make up illnesses so I could stay home. The teachers either weren't aware or didn't care. I flew under the radar because I performed so well academically.

In secondary school I worked out how to be popular and made it my mission to have a large group of friends, so I enjoyed it a lot more. I remember making friends and being popular was something that took conscious effort, and I was obsessed with succeeding. I was also obsessed with my appearance, which I linked to being popular. This has had a lasting detrimental effect on my well-being over the years.

I had severe insomnia in my teens – I couldn't sleep because my mind was constantly racing – and my disorganisation was extreme. I would turn up to lessons without my books and stationery, usually late. I lost everything and relied on my friends for copies of assignments.

One day when I turned up to chemistry late (again), I arrived to find that the class and the teacher were making bets on what time I would show up. We all laughed. The teacher was always baffled as to how I could maintain my grades, and I was particularly good at higher-reasoning questions. In one chemistry exam I was the only student in the class to get a very difficult question correct. The teacher asked me to explain how I did it and I had absolutely no idea.

There was no awareness whatsoever of ADHD in girls in the 1990s when I went to school. I assume people thought all my faults came down to personality, as my faults formed part of my identity. I was a complete mess in my twenties. It was harder for me academically in university.

I passed, but I didn't really care about getting good grades unless it was in subjects I was motivated by, like anything to do with writing and my practical teaching subjects.

I think it helped that my mother was completely supportive of me as a person when I was growing up. She only ever celebrated anything I achieved and made me feel as though I was a special person who could do anything. Education needs to change to focus on the many strengths of neurodivergent people. It would also help if emotional literacy and intelligence are taught in schools. Supporting people to understand what is going on in their own minds will go part of the way in enabling them to seek help and understanding when they need it, which is often.

Bridget Young, head teacher at Holmewood, a school for neurodivergent children

PART 2: HOW TO BUILD A POSITIVE RELATIONSHIP WITH THE SCHOOL

We've heard about some very useful strategies schools could try out, but how do you get them to implement them? Some schools are willing to do so because they have the knowledge, but for others you need to be part of the process of coming up with ideas. And to do this it helps to have built a positive working relationship with the school, in particular the SENCO.

For this to happen, I think we need to put effort in as parents – to try to control our anxiety, to make reasonable demands and be aware that people are busy. Schools as well as parents and carers have been thrown into an impossible situation where they don't have the money to carry out what they have to do. So make the effort to have a positive relationship with the school.

If you can't achieve this despite your best efforts, escalate it to someone senior, but also recognise if your school is not going to work with you in a reasonable, communicative and open way, and consider moving if this is the case. If there is a bad culture towards SEND at the school, this chapter is going to be of limited use and you need to focus your efforts on finding a more inclusive school for your child.

But if you can work with your school, my best advice is not to complain too much. An old boss of mine, James, rarely made complaints (to others outside his team, I hasten to add), but when he did: watch out world. Observing it up close made me realise what an effective tactic it was – by holding his punches for the things that didn't matter, the impact was knockout when it did. He only acted when he was certain he was in the right, had evidence to support his position, and it was really important to him. Whoever had annoyed him would then leap to it, as the fact that he didn't often get cross added to the potency of his reaction.

James, who is sweary, brutally honest and right almost all the time (which he would remind me of frequently with a twinkle in his eye), often told me not to sweat the small stuff. It was good advice, and something I try to remember in my interactions with schools. Obviously this approach is not going to be right if your child is struggling and the school isn't doing what it should do – you can't silently bide your time while your child is distressed. But his general principle of not reacting to every tiny thing is sound. Though perhaps without the swearing.

Tips for forming a positive relationship with the SENCO

1 Don't overcommunicate – SENCOs are busy people and you don't want them to take you less seriously when you email.
2 Be concise, factual and polite. Don't moan, be personal or make accusations. As a wise friend once said to me, if you

are angry, people tend to only hear your anger, not what you are angry about.

3 If you are worried or upset about something (and assuming it isn't hugely serious), don't send a long email; instead ask for a chat: 'I wonder if we can have a word about something I'm worried about. Do you have fifteen minutes after school or on the phone on Thursday?' Speaking in person is more likely to get an honest rather than a defensive answer. Follow it up afterwards with an email confirming your discussion and what has been agreed.

4 It can be helpful to suggest action points, so you cut down on the school's thinking time and the SENCO simply has to forward the email. For example: 'My son is finding Spanish difficult and he tells me the teacher is not letting him have his movement breaks. If this is the case, can you speak to the teacher about why these are necessary and ask them to confirm with my son that he can have these breaks?'

An example of an effective email to the SENCO: specific, concise and opens the door for a collaborative conversation:

Dear Sue,

I am emailing as I understand Joe's TA was used in other classes on the following dates . . . The consequence of this has been that Joe has returned home extremely anxious on those days with long meltdowns on two out of the three occasions. I'm concerned about the impact of this, both for him emotionally and his learning. Could we have a chat about this today or tomorrow? Thank you.

Jessie

PART 3: WHAT TO DO WHEN THINGS GO WRONG AT SCHOOL

School may not always be plain sailing for your child, which is likely to mean more communication between you and the teachers to see what can be done. A good school should work with you to come up with solutions, in recognition that the best results happen when school and parents work together, with both parties sharing their knowledge of the child. As parents, it helps to build a relationship with teachers and the SENCO where they feel they can be honest with you because you won't overreact. This involves accepting that mistakes will happen and recognising the imperfect system we're all subjected to.

What to do if your ADHD child gets lots of detentions

ADHD pupils get a disproportionate number of detentions and internal seclusions, and spend more time in 'isolation booths' – where disruptive students are put facing a blank wall. Nowhere near enough consideration appears to go into the fact that all these punishments are far greater for a kid who needs to move and has a brain that requires constant stimulation, and that children with SEND tend to spend a disproportionate amount of time in these booths.

'ADHD kids are constantly in detention and told off, and that's no way to live,' says Pete Wharmby. 'It causes trauma, and chances are they are doing their best and may hate themselves for forgetting something – again.'

If your ADHD child is being given detentions for forgetting things, they are being punished for being disabled. 'You have to go big on this, I think – point out that your child has difficulties with executive function, which manifests itself as forgetfulness, as part of their disability,' says Wharmby. 'And that the school

215

is not adhering to the Equalities Act, which obliges them not to disadvantage a child for behaviour related to their condition.'

Taking a child out of school

School is meant to be a place where a child feels happy (most of the time) and safe – and if those two things are gone, it's very hard to learn, never mind the consequences for a person's mental health. The rhetoric you hear a lot from schools is that children need to be in school no matter what, but if an adult was becoming mentally unwell because of their working environment, a doctor would sign them off.

'What we hear from adult neurodivergent people is they can be really traumatised by school, and this has consequences that can last a lifetime,' says a SENCO who wishes to remain anonymous. 'I would say to a friend if their child was having trouble attending: be aware that a school needs to tick an attendance box. If school has become so traumatic that it is starting to damage them, I would take my own child out in a heartbeat.'

This is no denying it's incredibly important to receive an education for all sorts of life chances, but there are too many neurodivergent adults who are very highly educated but whose confidence and self-esteem were destroyed at school, so they have not been able to convert their education into a fulfilling career or life. Had their parents known the lifelong damage that school – and being bullied – was doing, they might have made different decisions about the importance of sending their child there every day.

When my son first stopped being able to go to school at the age of eight, I knew I was going to have to deal with big conversations with the school and local authority about what we should be doing. There was pressure for me to work out how we were going to move forward, and I felt like it shouldn't be me, because I was the person in the middle who was juggling everything. I didn't feel equipped to be in the driving seat. The initial stages of trying to get him back into school left me frazzled. Helping him manage his overwhelming emotions and the fallout from the trauma meant I woke up stressed and I went to sleep stressed.

But then I realised around that time that I do know what's best for him and I should be driving this. It was him seeing a neurologist that made me realise we would stop trying for school – he was having so many migraines because of the stress and I realised this was all now having a physical impact on him. Once I made the decision he wasn't going back to mainstream school, and we would home-educate, I had a wobble after. I was scared about what I had done – had the genie left the bottle?

**Jess Wilson, senior SEN officer at MindJam,
an online mentoring company**

Burnout

There are an increasing number of neurodivergent kids burned out from school, and my son M is one of them. Noelle Faulkner, an Australian journalist, wrote about her ADHD burnout, and her description in a *Guardian* piece published in 2020 is better than anything else I've read. She said it left her feeling like her brain 'had been tossed into a washing machine, and all of the delicate bits that made it sparkle had dissolved'. She added, 'Everything took three times longer than it should have . . . "I can't keep it up any more," I said wearily. "It" being life. I wasn't suicidal; I was chronically overwhelmed.'

I think of burnout as a type of neurodivergent nervous breakdown. And based on M's experiences of school refusal, it doesn't come out of nowhere: you are seeing meltdowns at home that are becoming more frequent and distressing in their intensity, picking up an angry or upset child from school more frequently. I found the moment I acknowledged he was not able to attend school – and I wasn't prepared to put him in an overwhelming situation without the right support – was followed by relief. I hadn't fully realised the enormous stress that forcing him to go, and dealing with the after-school meltdowns, was causing us all.

I found it helpful to think how I might feel if work had caused a breakdown in me, in order to understand what had happened to him at school and the process of helping him get better. I'm certain I would not be having an Instagram-worthy breakdown – by which I mean doing the mindful activities social media tells us to, such as meditation, keeping a gratitude journal and going to the gym; instead I would be lying on a sofa all day mindlessly watching Netflix, joylessly scrolling social media and blowing my stack over tiny things until my brain was less fried. If someone suggested I went back to work 'just for five minutes' in this early phase, or scheduled a quick Zoom call to speak to my boss or colleagues before I felt ready, I would feel tremendous anxiety. I also thought of what the ingredients would be to cause me to break down – constant stress, intense feelings of failure – which gave me a clearer idea of the impact school had had on my son.

'You're not going to go from meltdowns and the trauma caused by school to being able to work with a tutor in a week's time,' says Jess Wilson. 'The recovery period may involve your child watching YouTube all day, or gaming, which they need to regulate. It can feel like you're neglecting them if they are not in full-time education and are on a screen full-time, but they should be allowed this as part of their recovery process.'

It took M around six months of being on a screen non-stop to start re-engaging with the world a little and before we could introduce a reduction in screen time (still a work in progress).

'My son used to read for pleasure all the time, but then after burnout he didn't read for over a year,' says Jess Wilson. 'It just felt too much like school. The only way I could get him to read was when we went on holiday. I bought everybody a new book. I didn't tell anybody, I just put them down on the table in the caravan. He stumbled across it, and he started reading it and didn't stop. We were literally at the beach, and he was walking along the sand reading it. I just kept removing the pressure.'

Jess works with lots of children in burnout and believes the quickest and most effective way out of it is to be patient, give the child back control of their life and let them follow their interests. For example, if school is keen for them to be given work straight away, tell the teacher your child isn't ready and that forcing them to work until they are better will only compound the problems. Then, when your child is ready, let them lead the process back to school. 'Children have so little control of even their bodies – in school, they are told they can't move, they have to wear this uncomfortable set of clothing. Some pupils are frequently being told off, and for them being offered the chance to lead what they want to do, it's such a relief.'

The duty to provide an education

Under Section 19 of the Education Act 1996, there is a duty on local authorities to arrange education for children of compulsory school age who are out of school due to illness (including anxiety). This is triggered if a child is out of school for fifteen days or more. Usually a school will apply to a panel run by the local authority to consider requests for

---

alternative education provision (e.g. a tutor coming to the child's home), but if this is not happening, the LA still has a responsibility to do this, so you should contact the director of children's services of your LA. IPSEA's website has some template letters that may be helpful. If you are working with CAMHS or a psychiatrist (who is perhaps overseeing your child's ADHD medication), having an email or letter from them confirming that your child is not able to attend school will be helpful.

Home education

'There's this idea that if you go down this route you have to give up your job,' says Jess Wilson. 'Some people do – your child's needs might be too high. But I do it and still have my job. Yes, it's a juggle, but people need to hear that it's not going to end your life. I didn't consider it for a long time because I thought it would be stressful and awful. But it's so much less stressful than forcing a uniform on a child who's got sensory needs and getting them into a classroom for a certain time in the morning when they've got PDA.'

Wilson managed to negotiate an 'education other than at school' package for her son's EHCP (also known as EOTAS). As part of this, the LA pays for tuition, occupational therapy, and online mentoring sessions with MindJam, who take a gaming approach to supporting neurodivergent pupils.

'You don't have to wait for your child to be broken to pull them out of school'

My children have always been home-educated and have never been to school. I know a lot of people end up home-educating because they have been failed by the school system, and often end up here after a lot of trauma and distress. I think it's important to know that you don't have to wait until your child is broken to pull them out of school. School is not compulsory, only education is. It's totally okay to follow your instinct if you feel that your child wouldn't thrive in the school system. Even if you feel your child would 'cope' or 'survive', that shouldn't be what we are aiming for – all children deserve to thrive.

I think it's also important to note that home-educators in the UK don't need to follow any set curriculum or stick to school hours if they do not want to, and that there are a wide variety of educational philosophies and styles out there to suit all sorts of families. The best thing about home ed is that you can follow your child's lead and facilitate learning in a way that suits them. For some families this might look like worksheets and online lessons and weekly museum trips, for others it might look more like forest school, play dates with friends and gaming. For neurodivergent young people it means that they can get more time to decompress from socialising, more control over what environments they spend time in, and more opportunities to follow their interests, hyperfocus and play to their strengths without things being arbitrarily timed or topics finishing when they would like to continue learning.

One of the things we do a lot is work together to review how well things are working, and make plans on how to change things and what to try next, as I think that working in collaboration with young people is really important. So if a certain maths app, workbook or website has become boring, what else can we find to use instead? Is there a particular topic they really want to learn more about? How would they like to do that? Is there anywhere in particular they would like to visit? I often 'strew' things – leave things in the home for them to pick up or look at if they would like to, without making a demand they do this – which reduces the pressure. Last week I bought a science comic about cats, as my youngest is currently really into some Warrior Cats graphic novels. I didn't ask her to read it, or present it as a lesson, but was like, 'Hey, I saw this comic about cats and I thought this one on the front looked really cute! I'm going to leave it here in case you want to read it.' She is now happily reading through that comic, which contains loads of scientific factual information, but she's accessed that in a really low-demand way that works with how her brain learns.

Kirstie McStay, community manager at Spectrum Gaming, the online community for neurodivergent young people

When is a special school appropriate?

'How I judge it is: is the child getting a good deal in mainstream?' says Heba Al-Jayoosi. 'Let's take two children with a learning disability as an example. One of them is pre-verbal and really happy. She goes out on the playground, has friendships and plays with other kids. And the other child is having a really bad time. He's having meltdowns daily. He has no friendships: his peers try to engage him with games, but it doesn't work. So on paper these two kids are the same but I would say the deal we're providing the second boy, no matter what we put in place, is a poor one. Friendships are very important in school – a lot of the time teachers look at the academic stuff, and we can all forget about the power of friendships. You can forget what it's like to be a child – and when you have no friends at school, it's miserable.'

Specialist schools offer a more tailored approach to teaching your children, which is likely to mean more movement breaks, fewer transitions, smaller class sizes, more adults on hand to support. They should also have more time for pastoral care – for helping young people with friendship difficulties, for example. Some of these schools offer fewer academic qualifications – partly as there may be time spent on other activities, such as learning to travel independently – but others work with neuro-divergent children who are capable of a mainstream curriculum but need a calmer, quieter environment. Some of these schools have traditionally been autism-specialist ones, but many pupils will have ADHD too, and some schools are now accepting pupils with just an ADHD diagnosis.

'School viewed my daughter as difficult'

Millie, who was in the local state school for the first years of her school life, really struggled. Nothing about school made sense to her, nothing was rational, it was all frustrating. School viewed Millie as difficult. She would disrupt a class, run out. She took up too much of everyone's time. Eventually there was a buddy assigned to help her, but they didn't understand autism or ADHD (not that we knew she had ADHD back then). So I would write out this sort of manual, if you like, for Camilla's needs – a list of the sort of things that triggered her and things that would help her. We eventually paid for her to go to a private school when she was nine or ten, as the local state school had no provision to cater to her educational needs. It wasn't easy to do that and as a family we worked really hard to afford this. Unprecedentedly our local authority paid for a learning assistant to support her there, so that her school life became less terrifying. I appealed to the Welsh Assembly to argue the case. I was in the education system – I taught photography and art at university – and this provided me with an insight into what wasn't happening for my daughter at school, how they were failing her, and I would write letter after letter to the local authority. The learning support would listen to the lessons and then explain the learning to Millie in a way that was accessible to her. It opened up the door to Millie's vast intellect and potential, her learning increased and her achievements began.

Sonia Pang, mother of scientist and author Camilla Pang

TL;DR

Three, two, one, pens down and eyes on me. Here is how to get the best out of school for your ADHD kiddo.

- Working best with the school involves not sweating the small stuff, building a trusting relationship with school staff and being mindful of their limited time.
- Rename fidget toys as 'focus aides' with your meetings with the school to underline their value.
- While there are many inclusive schools staffed with teachers going above and beyond, some schools are damaging ADHD young people.

- If your child is distressed at school, and the support isn't right or the understanding isn't there, think about if the school is the right place for them, particularly if the school has very rigid behaviour policies.
- Your child should not be getting punished for behaviour linked to their ADHD, and they should feel safe and happy a reasonable amount of time in school.

Illustration by M, age seven

11

ADHD and Girls

I have struggled to write this book – I'm typing this on my laptop as we drive down the motorway in France on holiday (my husband is at the wheel, I hasten to add). It has taken my editor getting firm with me to get the manuscript finished: the fear of displeasing someone has finally kick-started my brain into something approaching consistent focus. Well, by consistent, I mean I can sometimes work for forty minutes without wormholing through some very random websites, having completely forgotten what I set out to do.

The barriers to focus have not only been the existence of Google, however. There's having a child in burnout not able to go to school, the large amounts of admin involved around both this and sorting out his EHCP, and some difficult personal events to contend with, including the deaths of two people I was close to in one week.

But I have wondered if there isn't something else going on too. I loved pretty much every minute of writing my first book, *Autism*. I dived into the pool of autism and the water was warm. I powered down the lanes, absorbing all the research, perspectives and interviews; with every stroke I could feel my knowledge strengthening and my confidence in the subject growing. And while I was aware of the irony of writing about how to raise happy autistic kids while pretty much ignoring my own as I invested long hours in the book, home life was mostly happy too, as my fear of autism evaporated.

So I have asked myself repeatedly: why has writing this second book been so much harder? And as I interviewed ADHD adults, and their stories felt increasingly familiar, I started to wonder. I didn't just empathise; I knew exactly what they were talking about. I felt their words. I too have a brain that will only focus in very specific circumstances, leaving me feeling unproductive most of the time.

And then, during an appointment with my elder son's psychiatrist, shortly before she diagnosed him with ADHD, she asked me directly if I was aware how often I zone out. 'Er, yes, but doesn't everyone do that?' I asked. 'No,' she replied with a firm but amused gaze.

Obviously she was giving me quite a big clue as to what neurotype she felt I was. So I made an appointment for a private ADHD assessment (having discovered it was covered by my work health insurance) and noticed when I filled in their forms pre-meeting that I appeared to be ticking all the boxes. I now wonder if my first book went swimmingly because I was hyperfocusing on a special interest (autism), but this time I couldn't as there was too much going on at home, splitting my attention. I was completely overwhelmed by the pull between family and work, and was being prevented from diving into my monotropic pool and staying there. It was stressful and made me resentful; family life, which was already difficult at that time, became more so.

If I do get a diagnosis, it will probably come as a shock to those who know me. I assume I am not the type of woman people think has ADHD. While I'm a fidgeter and talk a lot and can go off on wild tangents, no one would ever describe me as active, let alone hyperactive. But learning about inattentive

ADHD has been a revelation. When I look at pictures of myself as a young child, I often look distant. Removed from the group, like I'm wishing I were somewhere else. Now I think: perhaps I *was* somewhere else. In my head, at any rate.

Interviewing many of the ADHD women in this book, what I've noticed is that initially I found it hard to identify their ADHD. It took time and direct questions for it to loom into focus. This is probably because women mask so effectively, but also because the whole way we conceptualise ADHD is based on male presentation. The stories these women share paint a picture of long-term difference, struggle and messy homes. The decade of self-discovery that is your twenties is often hard no matter your neurotype, but for these women (for us?), the toughness and the shame was magnified. Chattiness, disorganisation and a tendency to interrupt is less acceptable in girls than it is boys.

For the first appointment of my assessment, I clicked on the Zoom link only for the psychiatrist not to show up – he appeared to have forgotten about it. After ten minutes of frantically checking my emails, assuming I had got the date wrong (as usual), I felt that flood of sweet relief when I realised it wasn't me who had fucked up this time. This didn't stop me getting narky with the secretary, who gave me a new date, and I wrote it down in my diary . . . only to promptly forget about it entirely and realise, a month after the appointment should have happened, that this time I *did* fuck up. Turns out I'd written it down in the wrong month. I then emailed the secretary to confess, feeling embarrassed and wishing I hadn't been so cross about it the first time round.

So, wish me luck in this long process of finding out who I am in my late forties. In the meantime, I've been finding out more about ADHD women in general – and below is what I've discovered.

WHAT ADHD IN WOMEN LOOKS LIKE, AND HOW IT DIFFERS FROM MEN

Fidgety brain

It has been suggested that girls and women tend to have inattentive ADHD, rather than the hyperactive presentation. Essentially a fidgety brain rather than a fidgety body. The problem with internalised hyperactivity – another way of describing inattentive ADHD – is that it's harder to spot, and awareness is very poor. So it can take a long time for it to be picked up (if ever), especially as the owners of fidgety brains don't realise other people's minds aren't as active.

It is debatable whether girls really are more likely to be inattentive and boys more hyperactive, or whether these things are shaped by society's expectations of the sexes – i.e. that girls are given less leeway to be hyperactive, just as boys are given less permission to cry. But bear in mind it's not even clear at the moment if the subtypes that the *DSM-5* currently uses are a real thing. Potentially people just appear hyperactive and inattentive at different stages of their lives, on different days or in different environments.

ADHD women look like neurotypical women

It is often said that women mask more effectively. The idea is that girls and women go the extra mile to cover things up compared with men, as ADHD is seen as even less acceptable in women than it is in men. Or it's possible that women are naturally better maskers. While I don't know how on earth you measure people's masking, given that the maskers themselves often don't know the extent of what they're doing, it is easy to imagine that ADHD girls and women experience more social judgement. We're not supposed to be bad at hoovering, forgetful when it comes to people's birthdays or rubbish at repairing a social schism. By this logic, the upside will be that as the world becomes less sexist, girls and women will feel less pressure to mask.

WHY ARE SO FEW WOMEN DIAGNOSED?

Since ADHD was first formally defined (albeit under a different name) in the 1980s, far fewer women than men have been given a diagnosis.

The reason for this gap is that what we know as ADHD is male ADHD (more specifically white male ADHD). For decades, if not centuries, all the research was done on white boys and men. In the case of women, we weren't even adequately included in any kind of research until the 1990s; the first long-term study happened in 2002.

So if you conduct research for the most part exclusively on white boys for decades, then create a diagnostic framework around this skewed evidence base, you are not going to spot women (or anyone of colour, whatever your gender). And then the guidelines and training based on the research on white boys and men simply compounds the problem.

Patricia Quinn, a US-based paediatrician who has done research in this area, has found that ADHD women have higher rates of comorbidities (which means there are two or more conditions present at one time, such as depression and eating disorders, as well as the ADHD). This makes diagnosis more difficult, since it is often assumed that their problems are just mental health, or the mental health difficulties cloud the ADHD (depression can also play havoc with executive function).

But it's likely that women aren't just more likely to have more than one condition. Instead the mental health problems are *caused* by undiagnosed ADHD. As it's not identified, we roll down hills in the snow, gathering up diagnoses as we go, ending in big white complicated balls by the time we get to the bottom.

Some very depressing research carried out by the NU Hospital Group in Sweden in 2021 has suggested that girls have to reach a 'higher burden of emotional problems' to be referred for assessment. This is put down to the fact that girls are often less noticed by teachers. As the Australian journalist Noelle Faulkner describes it writing in the *Guardian*, 'Even though my neurodiversity has sometimes made me the loudest person in a room, because I was a woman, nobody noticed.'

There is a gender bias among teachers and professionals too, put to the test by two Australian academics, Jeneva Ohan and Troy Visser. They asked parent and teacher participants to read a vignette describing a child displaying symptoms of ADHD. Half the participants believed it described a boy and the other half a girl. Participants were then asked to rate their likeliness to recommend or seek services for the child described. Both teachers and parents were less likely to seek or recommend services for girls than boys.

There may also be an issue of women internalising more. And as is always the case, the kids who internalise their problems – who quietly die inside rather than throw a chair around the room – get less support and are identified later.

Two women on what it's like to have ADHD

'All these crazy women narratives are describing women with ADHD'

There are a lot of stereotypes that are essentially describing inattentive ADHD: 'She's away with the fairies! Oh, she's so dizzy!' Or there is the other side of it, to describe difficulties with emotional regulation: 'Oh, she's hysterical! Oh, she's a nutcase.' All these crazy woman narratives that are just really dismissive.

What I do think is consistent is that most ADHD women struggle with rejection. A friend once teased me about how I can't handle it, and have to be invited to everything, and I was really hurt by that. But then I knew there was truth to it – why do I get properly upset and rejected if I'm not invited to all the parties, when I don't even want to go to all the parties? I guess it also goes back to childhood, when you weren't invited. I am now working hard to remind myself that our reactions to rejection can be disproportionate, and to try my best not to act on these feelings in the heat of the moment. This is still very much a work in progress.

Kirsti Hadley, inclusion consultant and speaker on ADHD and autism

'I'm grieving for who I thought I was while trying to find out who I actually am'

I went to an all-girls school. I masked a lot to try to fit in and I did a lot of things that the real me wouldn't do.

233

As I've got older, I feel like I'm myself again. It has been an emotional process, almost like I'm grieving for who I thought I was while trying to find out who I actually am.

I can burn myself out as I overwork myself and I don't know when to stop. My social battery quickly runs out and I'm always juggling many things, but then, if I'm not doing loads of different things, I beat myself up for not being productive enough. My mind is always racing. There's so much I want to do, and there's so much I want to learn. I love collecting facts and information that can help me and others. It's like my brain never stops. It's just always tick, tick, tick, tick, tick, tick, tick.

School wasn't great for me, despite being academically bright. I started reading Harry Potter to myself at the age of four and was always in the book corner reading at primary school. At secondary school I found it hard to focus and I struggled with the social aspect of it. There was a lot of bullying in the first two years, so I changed the way I was, to stop getting picked on, and I started masking more intensively. Being one of the popular girls gave me some protection, though to be in with them I had to behave badly and do things I felt pressured into doing. The choice seemed to be either to be a villain or victim.

I remember always being told off for talking in class – I couldn't stop because I was so understimulated. I would get moved and then I would still talk to whoever they moved me next to. I asked the teachers if I could listen to music while working, because I couldn't concentrate with everybody else talking or doing stuff. Most said no, though a few let me listen on my headphones. I'm really hypersensitive – I can hear sounds other people can't hear and smell things others can't smell. I get distracted very *easily. I passed English and got an A because I've always loved to read. I also passed my other subjects, but I didn't get the grades I was predicted because I used to skip school quite regularly and this upset me because I know I probably shouldn't have done that and I wanted to do well.*

The person I was trying to be was very extroverted. She was the class clown and made a lot of jokes. I felt like if I made people laugh, there was less chance of being rejected. I used to talk a lot and overexplain. I still do this now, but I'm more self-aware and catch myself when I'm doing it.

I've always felt different. I have a lot of empathy and compassion but have been told I'm very blunt. I mean well, and I try to be less blunt, but I sometimes think, 'This situation is black and white – why are you making it grey?'

Shanelle

TL;DR

Scatty, away with the fairies and daft: the lowdown on female ADHD.

- There are a lot of women who are ADHDers and who mask very effectively.
- Women are thought to be more likely to present as inattentive (away with the fairies) rather than hyperactive.
- Women are far more likely to have their ADHD missed at school and not receive appropriate support at school.
- Often ADHD girls' problems present themselves when the social dynamics of school get more complicated and the

parents are able to scaffold less at secondary. At this point, difficulties with organisation become more apparent.

- At the moment, for every one woman or girl with ADHD, three boys or men are diagnosed. It is likely this will change over time, possibly to become 1:1. The whole way we see ADHD is actually male ADHD, and society or genetics moulds girls to present differently.

Conclusion

When my elder son was diagnosed as autistic, I feared what this meant and desperately wished that he weren't. I used to see ADHD kids and think: their lives don't seem too bad. They seemed sociable and confident. Compared with my anxious autistic kid, sitting on the periphery of neurotypical life, ADHD seemed like the less serious condition of the two.

Now, after writing this book, I don't see it this way at all. Not only do ADHD children and adults have a similar level of challenge, but they are getting less specialist support and under-standing.

We minimise the challenges – and positives – of ADHD as it is even less understood than autism, and its cause is less progressed. Where is the major national ADHD charity – the equivalent to the National Autistic Society – that represents the interests of ADHD children and adults and lobbies politicians on their behalf? Where are the ADHD specialist schools? Why does the government not formally record figures for ADHD, as it does for autism, which is less common? Where is the ADHD political community helping shape the conversation in the same way the autism one does?

In those moments when I had to chase up yet another ADHDer for a response, I amused myself by wondering if it's because the ADHD community is just too executive-functionally challenged

237

and frazzled to do any of the above. But more seriously, it feels like it's because ADHD has been linked for so long with naughtiness that none of these things has happened. Perhaps, too, society doesn't feel it has to change when the ADHD person can simply pop a pill and fit in.

I wrote this book to better understand my son and to know how to be a better parent. Ironically, I may have learned something key about myself, too, as I wait to start my own assessment for ADHD. Not for the first time, my children have helped me understand myself better.

But even though I may be the same neurotype as my son, it didn't mean I intuitively saw what was going on for him. So, M: when times were tough and you said I didn't know what things were like for you, you were right. I said (and really thought) I did, but I didn't.

Hopefully this book will show you how much effort I've made to change that, because I love you so intensely it sometimes hurts. Parenting you and your brother has made me face up to bits of myself I didn't want to look at, and I've become a better person for it. While I wasn't born equipped with all the skills you needed me to have, I've tried my best to learn.

I needed to better understand ADHD, and that is something we all need to do now. One way to do this is to look at the debt we owe to neurodivergent people. Hyperfocus is central to the ADHD experience – and it has no doubt enabled key advancements of the human race. There is no way of knowing how big the ADHD and autistic contribution to the moon landings was, for example, but it's reasonable to conjecture that it was significant. Partly thanks to the intense magic that is hyperfocus, as well as some good old-fashioned ADHD creativity and autistic attention to detail. This is just one example of how neurotypicals have been dragged into the future by a group they have consistently pathologised and demonised.

Conclusion

Things are changing fast, however, and the way younger people like my sons matter-of-factly disclose their ADHD makes my heart sing. But alongside this, we need some real understanding for those we love, so they can leave school less damaged, and use their hyperfocus in ways that benefit themselves, and possibly the rest of us too.

References

1: Defining ADHD

Diagnostic and Statistical Manual of Mental Disorders, 5th edn, revised (American Psychiatric Association, 2022).

'Attention deficit hyperactivity disorder: How common is it?' National Institute for Health and Care Excellence, last revised December 2024. https://cks.nice.org.uk

Dr Ned Hallowell, 'Ferrari Brain with Bicycle Brakes; in Conversation with Dr Tony Lloyd', ADHD Foundation, 8 April 2021. https://vimeo.com/534505225

Jillian Enright, 'The Social Model of Disability', 24 December 2021. https://medium.com

Dr Nick Walker, 'Neurodiversity: Some Basic Terms & Definitions', 2014. https://neuroqueer.com

Jonathan Mooney, *Normal Sucks* (Henry Holt & Company, 2019).

2: A History of ADHD in Ten People

Alexander Crichton, *An Inquiry into the Nature and Origin of Mental Derangement* (T. Cadell, junior, and W. Davies, 1798).

Diagnostic and Statistical Manual of Mental Disorders, 2nd edn (American Psychiatric Association, 1968).

V. I. Douglas and K. G. Peters, 'Toward a clearer definition of the attentional deficit of hyperactive children' in G. A. Hale and M. Lewis (eds.), *Attention and the Developments of Cognitive Skills* (Plenum Press, 1979), pp.173–248.

Dr Michele Novotni, 'The Controversy That Was Adult ADHD', *ADDitude*, 21 May 2024.

Fred Charatan, 'US parents sue psychiatrists for promoting Ritalin', *BMJ*, 321:7263 (2000), p.723.

3: Does My Child Have ADHD?

Diagnostic and Statistical Manual of Mental Disorders, 5th edn, revised (American Psychiatric Association, 2022).

Dr William Dodson, 'Secrets of Your ADHD Brain', *ADDitude*, 1 November 2024.

Jillian Enright, 'Rethinking Rejection Sensitive Dysphoria (RSD)', LinkedIn, 24 January 2023. https://www.linkedin.com/

Dr Edward Hallowell, '"Recognition Responsive Euphoria" or RRE', 11 June 2019. https://.drhallowell.com

Brandon K. Ashinoff and Ahmad Abu-Akel, 'Hyperfocus: the forgotten frontier of attention', *Psychological Research*, 85:1 (2021), pp.1–19.

Britney Nguyen, 'FTX CEO Once Played *League of Legends* in Pitch Meeting', Business Insider, 10 November 2022. https://www.businessinsider.com

4: The Diagnosis Process

Matilda Boseley, *The Year I Met My Brain* (Penguin eBooks, 2023).

Diagnostic and Statistical Manual of Mental Disorders, 5th edn, revised (American Psychiatric Association, 2022).

Fergus Murray with Sonny Hallett, 'ADHD and Monotropism', Monotropism, 2023. https://.monotropism.org

6: To Medicate or Not to Medicate

Robert M. Sapolsky, *Behave: The Biology of Humans at Our Best and Worst* (Penguin Press, 2017).

References

7: Executive Dysfunction

Marta Rose, Divergent Design Studios, www.instagram.com/
divergent_design_studios, 23 November 2021.

Peg Dawson, *Smart but Scattered* (Guildford Press, 2008).
Reprinted by permission of Guildford Press.

8: How to Help Your Child Be Happy

Maja Toudal and Tony Attwood, *Energy Accounting* (Jessica
Kingsley Publishers, 2024).

Lisa Lloyd, *Raising the Sen-Betweeners* (Penguin, 2025).

Natasha Hallam, 'Window of Tolerance', Autism Understood,
7 July 2023. https://.autismunderstood.co.uk

9: Negotiating with Your Local Authority

Department for Education and Department of Health and Social
Care (2014, updated 2024), 'SEND code of practice: 0 to
25 years'. Available at https://www.gov.uk/government/
publications/send-code-of-practice-0-to-25 (Accessed:
14/01/25)

10: Support at School

Education Act 1996, Section 19. Available at: www.legislation.
gov.uk /ukpga/1996/56/section/19 (Accessed: 14/01/25)

11: ADHD and Girls

Patricia O. Quinn and Manisha Madhoo, 'A review of attention-
deficit/hyperactivity disorder in women and girls: uncovering
this hidden diagnosis', *Primary Care Companion for CNS
Disorders*, 16:3 (2014).

Ulrika Klefsjö, Anne K. Kantzer, Christopher Gillberg and Eva
Billstedt, 'The road to diagnosis and treatment in girls and
boys with ADHD – gender differences in the diagnostic
process', *Nordic Journal of Psychiatry*, 75:4 (2021), pp.301–5.

References

Jeneva L. Ohan and Troy A. W. Visser, 'Why is there a gender gap in children presenting for attention deficit/hyperactivity disorder services?', *Journal of Clinical Child and Adolescent*, 38:5 (2009), pp.650–60.

Acknowledgements

To the professional team who helped us with M, particularly when times got tough, I'll always be grateful: Suzanne Salerno, what a great SENCO you are; to Sophie Jubb, for your brilliant advice and support; Miranda Burke, thank you for the Zooms and calls when we needed it most. Also thank you, H, for helping me so much while we navigated the EHCP minefield once again. To Jesse, Carmen, Adam, Milly and Buddy – M's second family – you have helped more than you will ever know.

To my family: my mum, Jean (who was there even when it was hard to be there), Abby, Jessica, Beau and Jodie, all the Pearts, Gazzy Jeff, Richard and Mary-Anne, thank you for all your love and help over the years. Thank you, too, to the best Kiwi cousins a woman could wish for (I'm talking about you, Bridget and Kim – Simon and Gabrielle, you're not so bad either). And Margaret, my lovely aunt whom I'm very close to, you've done so much for us and I'm enormously grateful.

Thank you, Helen Honey and Joanne Kennedy, for reading chapters and for being the perfect examples of top neurodivergent medical professionals (if only I could request to see only ND doctors – one day . . .) Thank you to Kirstie McStay of Spectrum Gaming for being patient with my many queries, and to Laura James for reading (and rereading my book) and regularly talking me down from the ledge and giving me your expert advice.

Acknowledgements

Thank you, too, to Sam Chown-Ahern, the talented illustrator for this book and a good family friend. I loved our tea and chats, thrashing out the ideas.

To my team at Orion – Jess Duffy and Jo Whitford, thank you for your skill and patience. And Jenny Spearing for helping me negotiate my contract and my best friends Fran, Caroline and Hannah, for always being there.

But most of all, M, thank you for (hopefully) being okay with me writing this when you come to read it. I have worried a lot about invading your privacy and hope I got the balance right. And thank you, equally wonderful E, for being so thoughtful and easy to love. And Eifion, as ever, there is no way I could do this without you (and your professional anal retentiveness); I love you very much, P, and always will.

Lastly, I wanted to acknowledge the loss of two people while writing this book, whom I miss a great deal. One of my very best friends, Conrad, whom I loved and whom I think of daily (Dijana, his wonderful wife, is the best too). And to Jasmine El-Doori, whom I was planning on interviewing for this book – how I wish I could have. You left me halfway through writing it, but will never stop being an enormous influence in my life.

Index

Index

Index

Index

Index

exercise 106–8
fish oils 106
non-stimulants 96, 97, 98–102
non-violent resistance techniques
141, 142, 145
norepinephrine 95–6, 99–100, 106,
107
Novotni, Michele 19–20

occupational therapist (OT) 47, 170,
171, 173–4, 177
OCD (obsessive compulsive disorder)
37, 53
omega-3 supplements 106
Omer, Prof Haim 141
online gaming 158–60
organisation (executive dysfunction)
120
outcomes, desired (SEN support)
177
'overdiagnosis' 20, 52, 54
overreactions 79–80, 147
overstimulation 81, 150, 151
overthinking 36–7, 38, 49

Pang, Camilla (Millie) 35–6, 84–5,
160–2, 223
Pang, Sonia 160–2, 223–4
Panizzon, Leandro 17
Panizzon, Marguerite 'Rita' 16–17
paralysis, ADHD 127–8
parasympathetic system 137
pathological demand avoidance
(PDA) 51, 68–72, 89
PDA Society 71
people-pleasers 41, 155
perfectionism 41, 124, 127
persistent desire for autonomy 51,
68–72, 89
ping-ponging brain 35–8
planning and prioritising (executive
dysfunction) 119
Pollnow, Hans, 'A hyperkinetic
disease of infancy' 15, 18
positive, seeing ADHD as 83–4
positive relationship (with school)
212–14

practical strategies (for school)
adapt the environment 205
allowing stimming and fidgets
200–1
be prepared to explain things more
than once 204
create a menu of tasks 202–3
deal with things in the moment 206
eat the frog 206
give ADHD kids more than one
thing to do at a time 202
keep things moving 208
movement and brain breaks
199–200
no way can you do that! 206
normalise a child zoning out or
finding it hard to focus 203–4
provide frequent positive feedback
208–9
rewards/motivations 206–7
understand executive dysfunction
203
understand what ADHD
productivity looks like 204–5
use music 207
work with special interests 201
private reports 186–8
procrastination 39–40
professional reports, value of 186–7
psychiatrists 2, 18, 58–62, 90, 99,
102–3, 228
psychologists see educational
psychologists (EPs)

Quinn, Patricia 231

racing thoughts 39, 126
racism 82
recognition responsive euphoria
(RRE) 41–2
rejection, extreme sensitivity to 40–2
rejection sensitive dysphoria (RSD)
40–1, 101, 105, 153–5
what you can do to help with 154
reminders 122, 126–7, 138
report, diagnosis 61–2
restlessness, marked motor 15

Index

Index